On the Wallaby Track

Essential Australian Words and Phrases

Laine Cunningham

On the Wallaby Track
Essential Australian Words and Phrases

Copyright 2016 Laine Cunningham

Published by Sun Dogs Creations
Changing the World One Book at a Time

Cover Design by Angel Leya

ISBN: 9780998224046

All rights reserved. No part of this book may be reproduced in any form or by any means, electronic, mechanical, digital, photocopying or recording, except for the inclusion in a review, without permission in writing from the publisher. Thank you for supporting authors and a diverse, creative culture by purchasing this book and complying with copyright laws.

Praise for Laine Cunningham's Books

"Laine Cunningham combines tenacity and courage along with profound insight. Her bravery is contagious. I keep Laine's books on a special shelf in my library, referring to them when I need inspiration."
—Pamela King Cable, Author, *The Sanctum* and *Televenge*

"The fact that Laine Cunningham spent six long months on her own in the Australian outback before writing this book leant a rich authenticity to her voice as she shared from her abundantly full, and talented, heart."
—Leah Griffith, Author, *Cosette's Tribe*

"Laine Cunningham gifts us with a collection of essays that tie into traditional Aboriginal stories, teaching us that Dreamtime Energy is a timeless energy that can address modern issues with love and relationships, friendship and community, illness and joy. Each of these stories stem from myths but Laine's presentation of the stories or myths proves more enlightening on how to live in peace and love for all. She is our spiritual messenger bringing us universal truths from an ancient yet extant culture. Mesmerizing and meaningful and inspiring."
—Grady Harp, Vine Voice, Hall of Fame Reviewer

"The best part about these short stories is that they give us a glimpse into a world many of us know little about, Aboriginal Australia."
—R. Perron, Reviewer

"Loved it! The traditional Aboriginal stories are fascinating reads. From reading Laine's book, it's easy to feel the sacredness in the Aboriginal culture. I hadn't felt this moved by Aboriginal spirituality since viewing Oprah Winfrey's visit to Australia's Uluru rock."
—V. Lathan, Reviewer

Table of Contents

ABOUT THIS BOOK	1
INTRODUCTION	4
A	6
B	11
C	26
D	34
E	40
F	42
G	45
H	50
I	53
J	55
K	57
L	61
M	64
N	69
O	72
P	75
Q	81
R	82
S	86
T	98
U	103
V	104
W	105
X	111
Y	112
Z	114
FREE SAMPLE FROM *WOMAN ALONE: A SIX-MONTH JOURNEY THROUGH THE AUSTRALIAN OUTBACK*	115
FREE SAMPLE FROM *SEVEN SISTERS: SPIRITUAL MESSAGES FROM ABORIGINAL AUSTRALIA*	119
FREE SAMPLE FROM *THE FAMILY MADE OF DUST: A NOVEL OF LOSS AND REBIRTH IN THE AUSTRALIAN OUTBACK*	125
ABOUT THE AUTHOR	130
ALSO BY LAINE CUNNINGHAM	130

About This Book

Aboriginal Words and Phrases

The traditional hunter-gatherer lifestyle of Australian Aborigines, along with the lack of domesticated pack animals, meant everything a person carried had to serve various purposes. Many of those uses are listed in the definitions that follow but these descriptions are by no means exhaustive.

When settlers arrived, an estimated 300 tribes were speaking over 500 different languages or dialects. The included words have found their way into relatively common usage in Australian English either as adaptations or place names. Although the names for traditional instruments would have varied by language group, certain ones have become nationally recognized for their traditional meaning and are used in common conversation.

The tribal language from which each word originated is not often listed because historically, little effort was made to honor the tribe from which the word came. Whenever possible, notes are made about actual and possible origins.

European Words and Phrases

Quite a few of the words and phrases used by modern Australians are holdovers from their originating UK usages. While Australian slang has developed into a rich collection of words and phrases, many common words and terms will sound like slang to visitors. These unique items have been included to clear away confusion and help visitors become comfortably engaged with Australian citizens.

Quotes

The quotations used to illustrate the usage of different words and phrases come from other works by the same author. These books are:

Woman Alone: A Six-Month Journey Through the Australian Outback. Of special interest to fans of Cheryl Strayed's *Wild* and Elizabeth Gilbert's *Eat, Pray, Love,* this memoir covers a spiritual sabbatical taken by Laine Cunningham.

At twenty-seven years of age, she seemed to have it all: tons of friends, a college degree, plenty of all-night parties, and a secure job. Yet every morning she dragged herself through a life that was corporatized and overly industrialized, a life that falsely glamorized everything she was supposed to want.

Guided only by a map pulled from an old copy of National Geographic, Laine camped in the Australian Outback for six months...and she did it alone.

Told with wry humor and sparked with suspense and warmth, *Woman Alone* conveys a desperate search that became a journey of comedy and compassion in a landscape that brought her peace.

The Family Made of Dust. This novel, which won two national awards, was called "One of the best novels in ten years" by the Hackney Literary Award Committee. Fans of Sara Gruen's *At the Water's Edge* will appreciate the suspenseful elements and fabulist mysteries. Readers of Sue Monk Kidd's *The Secret Life of Bees* will feast on lives that are so different and yet so similar to their own.

In the story, Gabriel Branch is a man displaced. Having lost his boyhood family to brutal adoption policies, his carefully constructed adult life balances on an emotional razor's edge. Then his best friend disappears in the vast Australian interior. The only clue is an Aboriginal artifact that leads Gabe back to the land of his birth.

As he searches for the friend who was like a brother, memories arise unbidden. Memories of the uncle who swung him up into a tree and called him Little Breeze. Memories of the mother he lost. Memories of the sickly sweet candy social workers used to steal him away to an orphanage where he and his brother were separated first by walls and then by adoption. Armed only with his totem animal, Gabe must find himself before a tribal shaman and the weight of his past crush him completely.

Seven Sisters: Spiritual Messages from Aboriginal Australia is a unique self-help book that received an honor in the *Carolina Woman's* Inspiration Award contest.

According to Australia's ancient cultures, all creatures and things emerged from the Dreamtime. The Dreaming is not just a collection of lore or a long-ago time; it is a living energy that flows constantly through the universe. It is then and now, divine and human, spirit and law.

Because the energy is as vibrant today as ever, the ancient stories retold in this book show us how to survive in a harsh world and how to thrive in our souls. *Seven Sisters* harnesses the Dreamtime energy by pairing these stories with essays that address today's challenges.

For readers of *The Secret, A Course in Miracles,* and Paul Coelho's works.

A free sample from each of these books is included at the end of *On the Wallaby Track.*

Further Reading

On the Wallaby Track is part of a series that offers unique, fun, and fascinating information about Australia. The other titles are:

18,000 Miles: An Australia Travel Guide Companion to Woman Alone is packed with practical tips and advice for anyone interested in their own Australian walkabout.

Amazing Australia: A Traveler's Guide to Common Plants and Animals. The entries are curated to provide readers with a broad understanding of the most common and the most unusual flora and fauna...including the dangers associated with certain plants and animals.

Fairy Bread and Bush Tucker: Surviving a Gastronomical Adventure in Australia (With Recipes). From the disgusting to the sublime, this book tells you everything you need to know about the odd quirks of Australian cuisine, experience the best wild foods, and avoid entrees that aren't worth the effort.

Recipes are provided for a number of dishes; when the original ingredients are hard to find outside of Oz, close substitutions will bring Australia to any table.

Introduction

Australia is a land unto itself. Its culture is surprising and its people wonderfully welcoming and warm. Many travelers who speak English expect to have an easy time whether they visit for a few days or a few months. But between the strong accent, Aussie slang, and words garnered from their United Kingdom-based history, understanding their particular form of English can be a challenge.

At one point, I spent six months camping alone in the Outback. During that time I visited a number of cities and small towns. For the first thirty days, I was lost. A lifetime of travel has honed my ability to understand unusually thick accents but in Australia, I honestly understood only half of what I heard.

The accent was only part of the problem. The other was the heavy use of slang words and terms mixed liberally with words and phrases that originated in the United Kingdom. Add to that my own accent, which was lazy, consonant-slurring American mixed with German vowels, and the Aussies had a hard time understanding me!

A few weeks into my journey, I went to a restaurant in Adelaide to dine on kangaroo steaks. When the waitress took my order, I asked for a glass of water.

"What did you want to drink?" she asked.

"Water," I said again, which was pronounced *wood-der.*

"Sorry, love. What was that?"

"I would like a glass of water," I said slowly, as if the extra words might help.

At this point the waitress fell silent with her pencil poised over her notepad. We stared at each other for a long minute. We both knew this was going nowhere. The menu didn't list water as an option, so I couldn't just point like you might when you don't speak the native language.

I racked my brain to find another way to ask for water but the only thing I could come up with was H2O. And, sorry, asking for a glass of H2O would sound like I thought I was talking to an idiot. So she and I remained in our silent communion until a guy at the next table leaned over.

"Wu-tah," the guy said in his fair dinkum Aussie accent. "She wants a glass of wu-tah."

I got my water. I also made a mental note to always use the Aussie accent for that word, which tends to be important for anyone heading through the desert.

During the following months I deciphered, word by word and phrase by phrase, just what the heck people were saying to me. I also adjusted my speech so that certain words were always pronounced in the Aussie way to ensure that I got the supplies I needed at each outpost.

By the time I hailed a cab back to the airport in Sydney, I shocked the cabbie by telling him I was going home to America.

"You're a Yank?" he asked. "Your accent is so thick I swore you were straight out of the bush!"

Well, I was, in a way. Six months can change you a lot. But since most people can't spend six months figuring out the language, I wrote this book. *On the Wallaby Track* contains most of what you'll need to eat, sleep, and survive in the beautiful and astonishing country called Australia.

Enjoy this book, and enjoy more of your time Down Under!

A

Aboriginal creole: A natural language that developed from a mixture of several languages, in this case tribal dialect/s and English (see *Kriol* and *pidgin*).

> *An Aboriginal woman named Melody paused to chat and soon beckoned me to her table to meet her friends. They spoke Aboriginal creole, a mix of English and local tribal languages.*
> Woman Alone

Aboriginal flag: The official flag of the Australian Aboriginal nation (see also *red, black and gold*).

> *The Aboriginal flag consisted of a field of black for the people, a block of red for the earth, and a yellow circle at the middle for the sun.*
> Woman Alone

Aboriginal reserve: A parcel of land ceded back to an Aboriginal tribe. The practice, begun in the 1800s to segregate Aboriginal peoples, developed into the ability to practice self-determination under the 1983 Aboriginal *Land Rights* Act.

> *He would wear the tires down to the rims and the rims down to the axles. He'd barge onto every cattle station and Aboriginal reserve, and he'd keep looking even after Rob went back to his own life.*
> The Family Made of Dust

For more information, see *18,000 Miles.*

Aborigine: The indigenous peoples of Australia have no common name for themselves. Like Native Americans, they referred to themselves using words that meant "people" or "human beings." The common term Aborigine is capitalized out of respect.

Acacia: A large genus of trees and shrubs in the Mimosoideae subfamily; also called *wattle*.

> *Rob described acacia blossoms glittering in seasonal swamps and wildflowers that roared across the ground in waves of blue and pink.*
> The Family Made of Dust

For more information, see *Amazing Australia.*

Acacia seeds: A small seed from the *acacia* or *wattle*. Traditionally used as a food source by Aboriginal tribes.

> *In times of famine, Aboriginal people knew that ants gathered enough tiny acacia seeds to make a meal.*
> Seven Sisters

For recipes, see *Fairy Bread and Bush Tucker*.

Ace: Excellent, at the top of its category.

Act the goat: To clown around; to do something stupid.

A few roos loose in the top paddock: To be less than fully aware or intellectually engaged; also to be crazy.

> *"I know he seems to have a few roos loose in the top paddock but he's a good mate."*
> The Family Made of Dust

Afters: Dessert.

For recipes, see *Fairy Bread and Bush Tucker*.

Aggro: To be aggravated; named for a cranky hand puppet on a popular television show.

Alaye: (Aboriginal.) (Imperative.) Look out. From the Arrernte language.

> *Then Andy's voice, urgent and young, cried,* "Alaye!"
> The Family Made of Dust

(the) Alice: Alice Springs, a city in the Northern Territory.

> *After a life spent between two worlds, Billy had traced his family back to the Alice.*
> Woman Alone

For more information, see *18,000 Miles*.

All froth and no beer: Vacuous; of no substance.

All piss and wind: Braggart.

All wool and a yard wide: True; trustworthy.

Amber fluid: Beer, the lifeblood of Australians, their culture, and their economy.

> *Marie enjoyed her usual glass of Irish cream, I imbibed bourbon and cola, and David saved the Australian economy by slugging back endless beers.*
> Woman Alone

For more information, see *Fairy Bread and Bush Tucker*.

Amen snorter: Preacher.

Ancestor: Ancestor spirit, the *creator spirits* of Aboriginal mythology.

> *Wherever their feet pushed up mounds, mountains arose;*
> *wherever the ancestors fought, the ground was trampled flat.*
> Seven Sisters

A nice piece of fat: Common saying heard around a grill whenever steaks are cooking to indicate the flavor that strips of fat add to the meat.

> *The crowd prodded different pieces to measure the trim with fingertips and eyes. Then they rejoined the group at the grill and proclaimed, "There's nothing better than a nice piece of fat."*
> Woman Alone

For more information and recipes, see *Fairy Bread and Bush Tucker*.

Anthwerrke: (Aboriginal.) (Place name.) Emily Gap, which lies east of *Alice Springs*. From the Eastern *Arrernte* language.

> *"He'd have me name the Dreaming sites visible from the hill.* 'Anthwerrke,' *I'd say, our word for Emily Gap."*
> The Family Made of Dust

For more information, see *18,000 Miles*.

Antipodes: On opposite ends of the earth; the South Pacific.

Ant's pants: Fashionably dressed; self-important.

ANZ: Australia and New Zealand; pronounced "ay-en-zed."

For more information, see *18,000 Miles*.

Anzac: A word derived from the acronym ANZAC, which stands for Australian and New Zealand Army Corps.

> *After the music and the spasmodic dancing got to be too much, we headed to the Anzac club.*
> Woman Alone

Apple eater: Someone from Tasmania; named for one of the state's main agricultural product.

Apples: Good, OK.

Apricots: Testicles.

Archerfish: A family of fish known for hunting land-based and airborne insects as well as small animals by shooting a stream of water from its mouth.

For more information, see *Amazing Australia*.

Argue the toss: To dissent from an agreement; from a gambling game called *two-up*.

Arnhem Land: A region in the Northern Territory near Darwin.

(A)Round the twist: Mentally imbalanced.

Arrernte: (Aboriginal.) A group of Aboriginal people in central Australia around *Alice Springs*; also their language.

> *Somewhere beyond the suburbs lay the Mt. Gillen ranges, a ridge formed when the wild dog had defended the Arrernte territory from the Dreamtime intruder.*
> The Family Made of Dust

Arse: Ass.

Arse over tip: To fall over.

Arvo: Afternoon.

Assimilation: The government's attempt to create an all-white population by taking tribal children away from their families (see also *Stolen Generations*).

> *His mother's love shored up his spine, and assimilation had left his guts rock hard and festering.*
> The Family Made of Dust

Aussie: Someone from Australia.

Aussie luck: The incredible good fortune that applies to any of Australia's citizens (see also *Lucky Country*).

> *The dying man had only a wide-brimmed hat and that fabled Aussie luck.*
> The Family Made of Dust

Aussie salute: Waving of hand across face to shoo away bushflies (see *bushfly*).

Australian as a meat pie: Traditionally or typically Australian (see *meat pie*).

Australian creole: See *Aboriginal creole* or *Kriol*.

Australian magpie: A passerine native to Australia with an exceptionally beautiful song (see *magpie*).

> *Where had Cockatoo's energy gone? Magpie said they had never known. Life always ran out like water evaporating from a billabong.*
> Seven Sisters

For more information, see *Amazing Australia*.

Auto club: A national group similar to the American Automobile Association that offers travel assistance and other services.

> *"The auto club wants fourteen hundred dollars to tow the van."*
> Woman Alone

For more information, see *18,000 Miles*.

Autogas: Liquid petroleum gas (LPG).

> *"You don't sell gas here?"*
> *A light flickered behind his eyes. "You'll be wanting autogas, yes?"*
> Woman Alone

For more information, see *18,000 Miles*.

Avo: Avocado.

For more information and recipes, see *Fairy Bread and Bush Tucker*.

Away with the pixies: Daydreaming.

Awning over the toy shop: Beer belly.

Ayer's Rock: See *Uluru*.

> *This was the site known to many as Ayer's Rock for the European explorer who had reported its existence to the newcomers.*
> Woman Alone

For more information, see *18,000 Miles*.

B

Back of beyond/Back of Bourke: The wilderness (see *outback*) or the <u>Outback</u>.

Backpackers: Travelers, frequently college-age but also older, who crisscross Australia carrying little more than what can fit into a backpack.

> *Kevin had fallen in with a group of backpackers. Besides belting out beery laughter that overpowered the music, they didn't do much.*
> The Family Made of Dust

For more information, see *18,000 Miles*.

Bag: To criticize.

Bagman: Hobo, wanderer; <u>swagman</u>.

> *"You just tell me what he needs."*
> *"Friends, for one. People his own age for a change. Not those stockmen who come through, the lot of them drifters and bagmen."*
> The Family Made of Dust

Bagman's gazette: The grapevine on which gossip is spread; derived from the gossip passed between <u>bagmen</u> or <u>backpackers</u>.

Baiame: (Aboriginal.) Also Baayami or Baayama or Byamee. The <u>creator</u> or "sky father" spirit of several tribes in southeast Australia.

> *Baiame, the lead sky spirit, arranged the world in a special way. He mixed certain animals with people in the desert regions and other animals with people along the coast. He divided saltwater fish from those that swam only in fresh water, and he sent insects to live in the trees and earth and air.*
> Seven Sisters

Bail up: To rob; to detain.

Bald as a bandicoot's tail: Hairless; from the rodent-like tail of a <u>bandicoot</u>.

Balls up: Mistake, snafu.

Banana bender: Someone from Queensland, where bananas are grown extensively.

Bandicoot: A small to medium-sized marsupial native to Australia and New Guinea.

> *But the Mulga-seed clan was jealous and tried to create a dingo*
> *using bones and the hair of women. Forked sticks became*
> *its ears, the tail of a bandicoot was tied behind, and*
> *the teeth of a mole lined its mouth.*
> The Family Made of Dust

For more information, see *Amazing Australia.*

Bandicoot gunyah: Makeshift or rickety shelter, a house that seems to have been built in a hurry (see *gunyah*).

Banged up: Pregnant.

Bang on: Exactly; correct.

Banjo: A skillet; a leg or shoulder of *mutton*.

Barbed wire: Also fence wire. More than sixty species of animals have been known to become entangled in barbed wire in Australia.

> *Gabe never knew there could be so much barbed wire in the world.*
> *Thistles of it bloomed on vines that subdivided*
> *the land and segregated the animals.*
> The Family Made of Dust

For more information, see *Amazing Australia.*

Barbie: A barbeque; also refers to the grill used during a barbeque.

> *"The family's gathering for a barbie tonight," she said.*
> *"You're more than welcome as my guest."*
> Woman Alone

For more information and recipes, see *Fairy Bread and Bush Tucker.*

Barcoo buster: Wind blowing inland in Queensland.

Barcoo rot: Tropical skin disease.

Bark painting: Traditional Aboriginal painting that uses a sheet of bark as canvas.

> *Today, Angus knew, he would begin a new bark painting. Red*
> *would stand for blood and the ghosts would be white. He would*
> *paint a possum in its nest with the ancestors gathered near. It*
> *would be his Dreaming to bring Rob home again.*
> The Family Made of Dust

Barmy: Crazy.

Barmy as a bandicoot: Really crazy (see *bandicoot*).

> *The couple backed away, clearly convinced that*
> *we were as barmy as bandicoots.*
> Woman Alone

Barney: Fight or argument.

Barrack: To cheer for.

Barramundi: Also barra. Asian sea bass.

> *I trailed a hand line in hopes of catching a barramundi, a popular*
> *entree, but the barra sulked beneath the heaving depths.*
> Woman Alone

For more information and recipes, see *Fairy Bread and Bush Tucker*.

Bathers: Swimsuit.

Bats: Crazy.

Bat the breeze: To chat.

Battler: Ordinary folks trying to make ends meet.

Bazzaland: Australia.

For more information, see *18,000 Miles*.

Beaut, beauty: An adjective to indicate that something is great; also an exclamation to indicate the same.

Belt up: (Imperative.) Shut up.

Bend the elbow: To drink alcohol.

Bent as a scrub tick: Crazy; see *scrub tick*.

Berko: Angry; berserk; crazy.

Bet like the Watsons: To bet excessively.

Better than a poke in the eye with a burnt stick: Better than a poke in the eye with a sharp stick; modification probably derived from Australia's seasonal bushfires.

Bible basher: Bible thumper; religious fanatic.

Big bickies: Lots of money (see *biscuit*).

Big land: A wide expanse of land; a country so large as to be incomprehensible.

> "*Big land out there, big sand and not much law.*"
> The Family Made of Dust

Big note: To brag.

Big OE: Big Overseas Experience; what young travelers are searching for.

Big smoke: City.

For information on specific Australian cities, see *18,000 Miles*.

(the) Big tour: Also the big walkabout. To undertake a tour of the entire nation by circling the coast and/or by running up through the middle of the country.

> *"Seems they're doing the big tour, out to see the whole country.*
> *But they don't do nothing but sit in the van all night."*
> Woman Alone

For more information, see *18,000 Miles.*

Bilby: Also rabbit-bandicoot. A type of small marsupial; one of the original two types is now extinct. (See *bandicoot*.)

For more information, see *Amazing Australia.*

Billabong: Ox-bow river; water left behind after floods recede.

> *When the dry season set in, the animals realized they had been*
> *given creeks and billabongs that held water*
> *only during the wet season.*
> Seven Sisters

Billy: Also billie. Any tin or bucket used to boil water for tea.

> *The billy crashed into the fire and steam rolled up from the sand.*
> The Family Made of Dust

Billy bluegum: *Koala*; from a koala's preference for hanging out in eucalypt trees (see *gum, gumtree*).

For more information, see *Amazing Australia.*

Billy lids: Kids.

(like) Billy-o: Also billio. Enthusiastically.

Billy tea: Hot tea brewed in a *billy*.

Bimbimbie: (Aboriginal.) (Place name.) A small town in New South Wales; name means "many birds."

For more information, see *18,000 Miles.*

Bingle: Fender-bender.

Birthing cave: One of many types of shelters where an Aboriginal mother might retreat to give birth.

> *"We just passed a birthing cave," Annie said. "It's really a space*
> *between the rocks. The ground is scooped away underneath,*
> *whether from erosion or to help the mother, I don't know."*
> The Family Made of Dust

Biscuit, bickie: Cookie or cracker; a *sweet biscuit* is a cookie, and a *savory biscuit* is a cracker.

For more information and recipes, see *Fairy Bread and Bush Tucker.*

Bite yer bum: (Imperative.) Shut up.

Bities: Collective term for any biting or virulent pest (i.e., insects, spiders, snakes) (see also *stinging nasties*); also the act of biting out of spite.

> *"Stop that!" she said. "No bities. No bities!"*
> Woman Alone

For more information, see *Amazing Australia*.

Biting flies: *Horseflies* or *March flies*, *stable flies*, black flies, and biting midges or *sand flies*.

> *Oh, he had griped about the flies and mosquitoes, worried about snakes and spiders, and had put up with more than his share of teasing because he always took a flashlight into the bush when he relieved himself.*
> The Family Made of Dust

For more information, see *Amazing Australia*.

Bitser: Mutt.

Bitumen: Asphalt; a road paved with asphalt.

> *I powered up the slope and surfaced on the bitumen.*
> Woman Alone

Blackbutt: A type of Myrtaceae tree native to southeastern Australia.

Black cockatoo: Also red-tailed black cockatoo, Banksian black cockatoo, Bank's black cockatoo. A large *cockatoo*, all black with red markings, consisting of five subspecies.

> *Further north bands of black cockatoos appeared. ... They were throwbacks to the shadowy jungles that once covered Australia and remembered a long-ago time when being black was not a burden.*
> The Family Made of Dust

For more information, see *Amazing Australia*.

(the) Black Line: An action during the Black or Tasmanian War during which attempts were made to eliminate Aboriginal Tasmanians.

> *One of their first efforts to wipe out the native population had been the Black Line, two thousand soldiers and civilians who tried to drive Tasmania's tribes onto a peninsula. After months of effort, two Aborigines were captured.*
> The Family Made of Dust

Black police: Also Australian native police. Police units composed of Aboriginal troops intended to utilize the indigenous peoples' tracking abilities and to assimilate the individuals.

> *Often they were given uniforms and membership in the black police force. No matter how shiny their buttons or how numerous their medallions, the splendor was as shrill as a mourner's grief.*
> The Family Made of Dust

Black swan: A large species of swan that is mostly black with white flight feathers and red beaks tipped with white.

> *Each crow gave up a few of its own feathers to clothe them. Ever since, Australian swans have been black with white wing tips.*
> Seven Sisters

For more information, see *Amazing Australia*.

Black Stump: The *Outback*; a rural area.

Black taxi: Government car.

Bleeder: Fellow, chap (see also *bloke, mate*).

Bleeding: A curse used as an adjective.

> *"These bleeding bus tours," he groused. "Cramped in a tiny seat for hours next to people I don't even like! All for twenty minutes or an hour at the site."*
> Woman Alone

Bleeding oath: Exclamation to indicate agreement.

Blimey: Exclamation to indicate surprise.

Bloke: Fellow, chap (see also *mate*).

> *While the older man worked steadily, the bowlegged bloke couldn't keep a proper watch.*
> The Family Made of Dust

Bloodhouse: *Pub*, bar.

Bloodletting: An event enacted during certain Aboriginal ceremonies, particularly the *man-making* ceremony and during funerary rites.

> *The Law demanded a bloodletting, the sorry cut, in exchange.*
> The Family Made of Dust

Blood pudding, blood pud: Strong-flavored sausage made from kidneys and blood.

For more information and recipes, see *Fairy Bread and Bush Tucker*.

Blood sacrifice: Wounds inflicted during certain Aboriginal ceremonies to connect participants to the *ancestor spirits*.

> *His scattered notes told the stories:* Blood sacrifice. Lizard Dreaming. Bushberry Woman. *Every one was a scrap of heritage scavenged by dogs.*
> The Family Made of Dust.

Bloodwood: Also desert bloodwood. A tree noted for the exceptionally red and thick gum it exudes when wounded.

> *The route took them over plains where blue mallee and desert bloodwood bent into fantastical creatures.*
> The Family Made of Dust

For more information, see *Amazing Australia*.

Bloody: Curse used as an adjective.

> *"What took you so bloody long?"*
> The Family Made of Dust

Bloody hell: Popular curse known as The Great Australian expletive.

Bloody minded: Stubborn.

Bloody oath: Exclamation to indicate agreement; stronger curse than *bleeding oath*.

Blooming: Mild curse, used as an adjective.

Blower: Telephone; in mining towns, the large suction machine used to clear slag.

> *Mark warmed up the blower, which was basically a giant vacuum bolted onto a flatbed truck.*
> Woman Alone

Blowie, blowy: Blowfly.

For more information, see *Amazing Australia*.

(like a) Blowie in winter: Slow, lethargic (see *blowie*).

Blow in: To drop by.

Blow in the bag: To test on a breathalyzer.

Bludge: To laze about; to mooch.

Bludger: Lazy person; moocher.

Blue: A fight or argument.

Blue duck: Disappointment; something that does not live up to expectations.

Blue heeler: A police officer.

Blue mallee: Also blue-leaved *mallee*. A small eucalyptus tree native to western New South Wales.

For more information, see *Amazing Australia*.

Blues: Police.

Blue tongue: Novice or unskilled; a general laborer at a sheep station; a ten-dollar note, derived from the currency's color.

Blue-tonged lizard: A large skink with a blue tongue.

> *The creatures celebrated by assigning every species to a suitable home. Death adders slithered into the central desert while blue-tongued lizards kept to the limestone plateau.*
> Seven Sisters

For more information, see *Amazing Australia*.

Bluey: A backpack; a traffic ticket.

Boab: A type of baobab tree with a swollen trunk shaped like a bottle.

> *I lazed away the afternoons under boab trees almost as thick as the car was long but even their dense shade provided little relief.*
> Woman Alone

For more information, see *Amazing Australia*.

Bob's your uncle: Exclamation to indicate understanding or that everything is fine.

Bodgie: Unskilled or of poor quality.

Bog: Toilet (see also *dunny*).

Bogan: Cad.

Boiler: Derogatory term for an elderly woman.

Boil the billy: To boil water for tea (see *billy*).

Bone pointing: An action that accompanies throwing a curse; from Aboriginal traditions (see *point the bone*).

> "A bone pointing doesn't always mean you'll die. It just means he'll try to kill you."
> The Family Made of Dust

Bonnet: The hood of a car.

Bonzer: Exclamation meaning great; a ripper of a joke; a good friend.

Boofhead: Idiot.

Boolaroo: (Aboriginal.) (Place name.) A suburb of the city of Lake Macquarie in New South Wales; name means "many flies."

For more information, see *18,000 Miles*.

Boomer: Male red kangaroo (see also *flyer, roo*); anything excessively large; an exaggerated lie.

> "Ian McCabe came, none too soon. Many boomers about."
> The Family Made of Dust

For more information, see *Amazing Australia*.

Boomerang: Check returned for insufficient funds (see also *boomerang (Aboriginal)*).

Boomerang: (Aboriginal.) Two types were invented. The most familiar is the returning boomerang, which has equal sides. The hunting boomerang was fashioned with one short side.

> *Then two brothers, heroes with a litany of exploits to their credit, heard about the woman. The brothers killed the dingoes with boomerangs and chased the woman from the country.*
> The Family Made of Dust

Boot: The trunk of a car.

Boots and all: Enthusiastic.

Booze artist: Alcoholic or heavy drinker.

Booze bus: Police vehicle carrying a breathalyzer.

Boozer: *Pub*; party; an alcoholic.

Booze-up: Wild party.

Bo-peep: To sneak a look at something.

Bora ground: Area where traditional Aboriginal ceremonies are conducted, especially the *man-making* ceremony.

> *If they lit a fire to drive away their fears, they would fail. If they fled the bora ground in terror, they would fail.*
> Seven Sisters

Bore: A well.

> *The meat kept well enough in a hollow log or weighted in the cool depths of a bore hole.*
> The Family Made of Dust

Boree: (Aboriginal.) Yelling.

Bore water: Water from a *bore*; the water tends to have a high mineral content that affects its flavor.

> *"I saw you drinking the bore water right off," she said, "but I didn't want to say anything. Thought maybe you liked it, you being a Yank and all."*
> Woman Alone

For more information, see *18,000 Miles*.

Bot: To cadge.

Bottlebrush: A shrub with cylindrical, brush-like flowers found in temperate regions that is widely used in landscaping.

> *Nor had he moved from the back porch where the sweet tang of the bottlebrush was heavy enough to veil his skin.*
> The Family Made of Dust

For more information, see *Amazing Australia*.

Bottler: Outstanding.

Bottle shop: Liquor store.

For more information, see *18,000 Miles*.

Bowerbird: Packrat; thief. From courtship rituals of male bower bird, which collects objects of particular colors to display on its mating ground.

For more information, see *Amazing Australia*.

Bowser: Gasoline pump; named for the American who invented it.

> *At the counter, the cashier talked around a wad of chewing tobacco. "That yer mate at the Bowser?" he asked.*
> The Family Made of Dust

For more information, see *18,000 Miles*.

(like a) Box of birds: To feel ecstatic

(like a) Box of blowies: Ugly (see *blowie*).

Boy's/girl's home: An orphanage that shelters boys or girls, respectively. Freighted with the history of Australia's genocidal *assimilation* policy.

> *When he realized the social worker meant to leave him with a strange* mperlkere *couple, he begged her to take him back to the boy's home.*
> The Family Made of Dust

Brangus: A breed of beef cattle.

> *Cattle ranchers tended to run Brangus, a hearty breed that crossed Angus with the tough Brahman.*
> Woman Alone

Brass razoo: Brass farthing; very little money.

Breakfast bird: Kookaburra, for the bird's raucous territorial calls at dawn.

> *Then Kookaburra began to sing her strange, stuttering call. The sound was like a chuckle that built to a rattling laugh. It clattered against rocks and echoed back from the cliffs.*
> Seven Sisters

For more information, see *Amazing Australia*.

Breakie, breaky: Breakfast.

> *"Cakes?" she asked. "You eat cakes for breakies?"*
> Woman Alone

For more information and recipes, see *Fairy Bread and Bush Tucker*.

Break it down: Exclamation indicating disbelief or awe.

Brewer's droop: Impotence caused by alcohol.

Bright spark: Cheerful or alert person.

Broken packet of biscuits: Something that looks good on the outside but is a mess inside.

Brolga: A blue-grey wetland bird of tropical and southeastern Australia and New Guinea known for its complex mating display.

> *While even an astonishing dancer might eventually be forgotten, brolgas continue to bring humans joy.*
> Seven Sisters

For more information, see *Amazing Australia*.

Brown snake: The *eastern* or common brown snake, native to Australia, Papua New Guinea, and Indonesia, is considered to be the second-most venomous land snake in the world.

> *On cattle stations hundreds of kilometers wide, engine trouble and the bite of the brown snake posed constant threats.*
> The Family Made of Dust

For more information, see *Amazing Australia*.

Brumby: Feral or wild horse.

For more information, see *Amazing Australia*.

Brummy: False; something that falls short of expectations.

Bubbler: Water fountain.

Buckley's chance, Buckley's: No chance at all.

Buffer: Elderly man.

Bug: A small, edible crustacean from Moreton Bay that resembles a large cockroach.

For more information and recipes, see *Fairy Bread and Bush Tucker*.

Bugalugs, buggerlugs: Term of endearment.

Bugger: Noun: A worthless person. Verb: To treat (someone) unfairly or to ruin (something).

> *"They'll make you think they need help and steal your petrol. Bugger you!"*
> Woman Alone

Bugger about: To fool around (see *stuff about*).

Bugger all: Absolutely nothing.

Bugger off: (Imperative.) Go away.

Bugle: Nose.

Bullamank: A remote area (see also *Outback, outback*).

Bulldust: Talc-like dust found in the *Outback*; a lie or tall tale; an exclamation indicating disbelief.

> *Bulldust, the red talcum powder that swirled atop the desert plains, became a pasty muck in the rain. ... Even machines spared the rough opal fields fell to ruin from the insidious dust.*
> Woman Alone

For more information, see *18,000 Miles*.

Bulldust artist: One who exaggerates.

Bullroarer: A slab of bone, stone or wood attached to a string; when twirled, it produces an eerie howl. Used during traditional Aboriginal ceremonies; also is a toy.

Bull's wool: False information; something meant to mislead.

Bum: Buttocks.

> *"Harmless," David added, "but annoying. And I know how Yankee women are! You'll pop him one if he pats your bum!"*
> Woman Alone

Bung: To place, to set (something) down carelessly; broken.

Bung it on: To be affectionate.

Bunyip: Mythological creature that lives in a *billabong*. Has been called Australia's Bigfoot. A bunyip makes a nuisance of itself by playing pranks like stealing the shoes campers leave outside their tents at night.

Bunyip aristocracy: Rural landowners (see *bunyip*).

Burger: A sandwich made with cold cuts. Only by ordering a hamburger will a hungry customer receive a sandwich made with a beef patty.

For more information and recipes, see *Fairy Bread and Bush Tucker*.

Bush: The wild and untamed Outback.

> *Some years ago, I spent six months camping alone in the Australian outback. Every night I cooked over an open fire as dingoes patrolled the bush.*
> Seven Sisters

Bush Baptist: Religious fanatic.

Bushbash: Off-road driving.

Bushberry: Also bush berry. The fruit of the blushwood tree. The seeds have recently been found to cure certain types of cancer.

For more information, see *Amazing Australia*.

For recipes, see *Fairy Bread and Bush Tucker*.

Bush cherry: Also native cherry or cypress cherry. A type of sandalwood endemic to Australia; the fruit of the same tree.

> *Bush cherry branches and gum leaves were heaped atop embers surrounding the bodies.*
> The Family Made of Dust

For more information, see *Amazing Australia*.

For recipes, see *Fairy Bread and Bush Tucker*.

Bushcraft: Survival skills needed to live for a period of time in the <u>Australian bush</u> or in the <u>Outback</u>.

> *Then a hulk of a man appeared. He was part of a special Australian military force trained in guerilla tactics and bushcraft skills.*
> Woman Alone

Bush dinner: Black tea, *mutton* and *damper*.

Bush fig: Also native fig. A small bushy tree that grows in central Australia, often in rocky gullies; the fruit of the same tree.

For more information, see *Amazing Australia*.

For recipes, see *Fairy Bread and Bush Tucker*.

Bushfly: The most tenacious, persistent, annoying, and irritating creature you will ever meet. The Aussies say that the Outback must be fun because fifty million bushflies can't be wrong.

> *Still, the comments buzzed in her mind like a horde of bushflies.*
> Seven Sisters

For more information, see *Amazing Australia*.

Bush guide: An individual with enough knowledge to guide visitors through the wilderness.

> *"Bush guide," Dana snorted. "I doubt he can fix a flat, let alone say much about the desert."*
> The Family Made of Dust

Bushie, bushy: Resident of the <u>Outback</u>; something authentically Outback in origin.

Bush meat: Also wild meat, wild game. Meats derived from the animals that roam free in Australia. Can include feral and invasive species.

For more information and recipes, see *Fairy Bread and Bush Tucker*.

Bush potato: Also rock morning glory. Edible tubers traditionally eaten by Aboriginal tribes; the plant that produces the tubers.

> *[T]he uncles brought a feast. Bush tomatoes and bush potatoes and witchetty grubs had been roasted on hot coals. The loin of a kangaroo dripped with juice and the drumsticks of a bustard let off a smoky steam.*
> Seven Sisters

For more information, see *Amazing Australia*.

For recipes, see *Fairy Bread and Bush Tucker*.

Bush raison: Also desert raison. A *bush tomato* plant; the dried fruit of the same plant.

For more information, see *Amazing Australia*.

For recipes, see *Fairy Bread and Bush Tucker*.

Bush telegraph: Grapevine.

Bush tomato: A small *solanum centrale* shrub; the fruit of the same shrub.

> *Wiry clumps of spinifex grass sprout from the plain, and the purple flowers of bush tomatoes promise a sweet harvest.*
> Seven Sisters

For more information, see *Amazing Australia*.

For recipes, see *Fairy Bread and Bush Tucker*.

Bush tucker: Wild food (see *tucker*).

> *One day all the men went hunting and the women and children left to gather bush tucker.*
> Seven Sisters

For information and recipes, see *Fairy Bread and Bush Tucker*.

Bustard: Large terrestrial birds that live in dry grasslands.

> *He thought of his uncle, and of how the bustard's bronze feathers had matched his skin.*
> The Family Made of Dust

For more information, see *Amazing Australia*.

For recipes, see *Fairy Bread and Bush Tucker*.

Butcher, butcher's hook: To peer closely at or to thoroughly examine something; rhyming slang derived in part from the *butcherbird's* hooked beak and its tendency to closely examine new items.

Butcherbird: A large songbird with complex songs.

> *The butcherbird roosted somewhere to the east.* Sweet pretty creature, *it called. The night did not respond.*
> The Family Made of Dust

For more information, see *Amazing Australia.*

Butcher's canary: Blowfly, derived from the fly's life cycle.

By jingo: Exclamation of surprise.

C

Cabbage patcher: Resident of Victoria.

Cackle berry: Egg.

Cactus: Dead; spoiled or broken.

Cakes: Pastry that looks like donuts right down to the hole in the middle made of heavy cake dough.

> "Yeah, donuts," she said. "I've heard about them. What are they?" ...
> "Those round thingies we saw at the bakery," I said. "The ones with the holes in the middle."
> "Cakes?" she asked.
> Woman Alone

Camel race: The annual Camel Cup takes place in *Alice Springs*.

> Gabe made room for his flier among ads for cattle stations, last year's camel race, hostels and hotels. A photo of Ian's face, a picture of his truck, and a list of his last known locations condensed all of his and Dob's and Rosie's feelings into shades of black and gray.
> The Family Made of Dust

For more information, see *18,000 Miles*.

Camooweal: (Place name.) A small village in northwest Queensland supposedly named for a surveyor who was the first to bring camels into the region.

For more information, see *18,000 Miles*.

Camp dog: Semi-tamed or fully tamed *dingoes*, mixed-breeds, or dogs brought by settlers that belonged to Aboriginal people or that hung around their camps.

> He sat absolutely still. Even as the mosquitoes drained his blood, even when the camp dogs sniffed his hands he did not move.
> Seven Sisters

For more information, see *Amazing Australia*.

Cane toad: An astonishingly large true toad introduced to Australia that endangers native species when they try to eat the poisonous creature.

For more information, see *Amazing Australia*.

Cannibal: In Aboriginal stories, a person or monster who consumes human flesh.

> *It was a child's song, one to ward off the cannibal who snatched up youngsters when they wandered too far from the fire.*
> The Family Made of Dust

Capsicum: Green or red bell pepper.

For more information and recipes, see *Fairy Bread and Bush Tucker*.

Captain Cook: A very close look or examination, derived from Captain Cook's early exploration of Australia.

Caravan: Trailer, fifth wheel.

Caravan park: A camping area, usually charging a fee, where individuals towing campers can hook up to power overnight.

> *That night would be the last I voluntarily passed in a caravan park.*
> Woman Alone

For more information, see *18,000 Miles*.

Cark it: To die.

Car park: A parking garage or parking lot. Every city has at least one car park set aside for used car sales where travelers can buy or sell cars.

> *My return to Sydney led directly into the dark and suffocating bowels of the King's Cross car park....*
> Woman Alone

For more information, see *18,000 Miles*.

Carpetbagger steak: Steak stuffed with oysters.

For recipes, see *Fairy Bread and Bush Tucker*.

Carpet grub: Child.

Carry on like a pork chop: To be silly or unreasonable.

Carry the mail: To buy a round of drinks.

Carton: A case of alcohol or other beverages.

> *"BPs! You buy carton BPs!"*
> Woman Alone

Caustic bush: A small tree that can grow in shrub form in Northern Australia. The name is derived from the burns the sap can cause on human skin.

> *"How about the caustic bush? It's a tender looking thing but if the sap gets on you, it burns like acid."*
> Woman Alone

For more information, see *Amazing Australia*.

Chalkie: Professor.

Charge like a wounded bull: To ask too much for a product or service.

Charm sticks: Sticks used to call up *Dreamtime* energy.

> *With them, he would make charm sticks to torment his enemies.*
> The Family Made of Dust

Chateau cardboard: Wine sold in a box with a foil bladder inside.

ChCh: Christchurch, New Zealand.

Cheeky: Forward; bold.

Cheerio: Goodbye.

Cheers: Thanks; here's to you (with raising of beer mug).

Chemist: Drug store.

For more information, see *18,000 Miles*.

Chew the cud: To ponder.

Chicken Rock: The spot on *Uluru* where many hikers turn back because the climb ahead is too steep.

> *From the parking lot, the journey looked neither high nor difficult. But a short distance up the slope was an area called Chicken Rock.*
> Woman Alone

For more information, see *18,000 Miles*.

Chilly bin: Cooler.

Chin wag: A long conversation.

Chip buddie: Also chip buddy. A greasy, salty, starchy combination of French fries (*chips*) with buttered white bread that is surprisingly addictive.

For recipes, see *Fairy Bread and Bush Tucker*.

Chippie: Carpenter.

Chips: French fries (see also *crisps*).

> *"I sweated my life away [digging] for potatoes when you could have bought chips?"*
> The Family Made of Dust

For more information and recipes, see *Fairy Bread and Bush Tucker*.

Chock: To kick.

Chock a brown dog: To relieve tension or aggression by doing something active.

Chockers: Full, from "chock-o-block."

Choice: Great; prime.

Choof off: To leave.

Chook: A chicken.

Choom: English person (see also *Pom*).

Chuck a wobbly: To tell a lie; to throw a tantrum.
Chunder: To vomit.
Cig, ciggie: A cigarette (also see *rollie*).
Clackers: Teeth.
Clanger: A lie; a shock.
(like the) Clappers: Quickly; frantically.

> *The entire time, his lips went like the clappers.*
> Woman Alone

Clap sticks: *Boomerangs* slapped together to keep time to music, as during a *corroboree*.

> *Musicians often accompanied the drone with click sticks, a modernized version of clap sticks or boomerangs.*
> Woman Alone

Claytons: A trick or fake.
Cleanskin: Unbranded cattle.
Clever man/woman: An individual well versed in harnessing *Dreamtime* energy.

> *"Clever men learn different ways of doing things."*
> The Family Made of Dust

Clicks: Kilometers.

> *I assumed I was having an allergic reaction and headed for the nearest hospital two hundred clicks to the north.*
> Woman Alone

Click sticks: Two sticks made of hardwood that are used to keep time to music, frequently that of the *didgeridoo*. Click stick were not traditionally used by Aboriginal people but were developed mainly for the tourist trade.

> *Smell the tang of eucalyptus trees and taste the cool water from a shady billabong. Hear the droning didgeridoo and the sharp click-sticks that accompany the songs.*
> Seven Sisters

Cloakroom: Toilet (see also *dunny*).
Clucky: Maternal.
Clued up: Well informed.
Cluey: Intelligent.
Coach: A bus.

> *The coach parked about twenty feet away, close enough that lathering any part of my body except my head suddenly became an uncomfortably erotic exhibition.*
> Woman Alone

For more information, see *18,000 Miles*.

Cobber: Friend.

Cockatoo: Any of the many species of parrot belonging to the Cacatuidae family.

> *Cockatoos crowded the trees and flipped their yellow crests like angry blooms.*
> Seven Sisters

For more information, see *Amazing Australia*.

Cockatoo weather: Sunny during the day, rain at night.

Cockie, cocky: *Cockatoo*; farmer, because both the farmer and the bird scratch about in the dirt looking for food.

Cockroach: A resident of New South Wales; derived from the exceptionally large cockroaches found there.

For more information, see *Amazing Australia*.

Cock up: A mistake.

Codswallop: A lie or tall tale.

Collymongle: (Aboriginal.) Long lagoon.

Collywobbles: Apprehension.

Come a cropper: To fall from grace; to make a mistake; to fall on bad times.

Come a guster: To make a mistake; to fall on bad times.

Come the raw prawn: To act naive (see *raw prawn*).

Commissioner: A police chief.

> *The Commissioner leaned against the counter. The move was calculated to set him at ease but Gabe knew his every word and gesture was being scrutinized.*
> The Family Made of Dust

Compo: Worker's compensation.

Conkleberries: Also conkerberry, bush plum. The fruit of a large dogsbane shrub commonly called the currant shrub, not to be confused with the bush currant.

> *They were as sweet as conkleberries.*
> The Family Made of Dust

For more information, see *Amazing Australia*.

For recipes, see *Fairy Bread and Bush Tucker*.

Coober Pedy: A city in South Australia.

> *But the weeks I'd spent in Coober Pedy showed me an Outback that was rough with a lifestyle that was rougher.*
> Woman Alone

For more information, see *18,000 Miles*.

Coo-ee: Outback distress signal. An annual coo-ee contest gives awards to callers who have the loudest and longest coo-ee.

Coolamon: (Aboriginal.) Curved piece of wood used to hold food or water, as a baby carrier, or to scrape the ground free of stickers.

> *Working as quickly as his stumpy arms allowed, he filled the coolamons with water.*
> Seven Sisters

Coolibah: Native tree with a mushroom-shaped canopy.

> *The morning sun pierced the coolibah and filtered through the bay window in the guest room.*
> The Family Made of Dust

For more information, see *Amazing Australia*.

Coolie bin: Cooler.

Corella: A subgenus of white *cockatoos*.

> *Ian lived in this region, in the wild spaces between outposts. Thanks to their friendship, Gabe knew the cockatoo and the corella.*
> The Family Made of Dust

For more information, see *Amazing Australia*.

Corkwood: One of four types of shrubs or trees with various traditional Aboriginal uses.

> *Corkwoods writhed from islands of spinifex and Flinders grass while figs fringed a nearby butte.*
> The Family Made of Dust

For more information, see *Amazing Australia*.

Cormorant: One of several types of water birds found in Australia.

> *This woman loved to dance. She added new moves every day by mimicking different animals. When she saw a cormorant spread its wings to the sun, she threw her arms wide.*
> Seven Sisters

For more information, see *Amazing Australia*.

Cornies: Corn flakes.

For recipes, see *Fairy Bread and Bush Tucker*.

Corroboree: Party; see <u>Aboriginal meaning</u>.

Corroboree: (Aboriginal.) Ceremony or celebration to mark a sacred event such as a child's coming of age.

> *Toward dawn, the corroboree was still going strong. The sun touched the horizon, yet the stars glowed like brilliant crystals.*
> Seven Sisters

Cossie, cozzie: Clothing; swimsuit, from "swimming costume."

Cot case: Bedridden patient.

Could kick the ass off an emu: Healthy, exuberant; from the <u>*emu's*</u> ability to kick and pummel enemies with its strong legs.

Couldn't give a continental: Couldn't give a damn.

Couldn't knock the skin off rice pudding: Weak.

Couldn't last a round in a revolving door: Weak, ineffective.

Couldn't pull a greased stick out a dead dog's ass: Weak, ineffective.

Couldn't run a chook raffle in a country pub: Incompetent; derived from the popularity of raffling off meat in <u>*pubs*</u> (see also <u>*chook*</u>).

(like a) Country dunny: Forlorn, alone (see <u>*dunny*</u>).

Crack onto: To make a pass at (someone).

Cradle rocker: A baby born in a hospital and therefore placed immediately into a cradle rather than into its mother's arms to be rocked.

> *She fixed me with a slow, easy grin.*
> *"I no cradle rocker, neither!" she said. "I not born in hospital."*
> Woman Alone

Crazy as white ants: Mentally unbalanced, derived from the behavior of termites (<u>*white*</u> or winged ants).

> *"We were waving our hats and shouting like we were as crazy as white ants!"*
> Woman Alone

Creator spirit: One of the <u>*ancestor spirits*</u> responsible for creating all living things and different places.

> *The Rainbow Serpent, a creator spirit known to nearly every tribe in Australia, often crawled atop Uluru to sun itself.*
> The Family Made of Dust

Crested pigeon: One of two Australian pigeon species to have a crest.

> *Voices, laughter and the call of the crested pigeon hung in the darkness.*
> The Family Made of Dust

For more information, see *Amazing Australia*.

Crikey: Exclamation of surprise.

> *"Crikey. Ya sure go through 'em fast. No wonder you're still single."*
> The Family Made of Dust

Crisps: Potato chips (see also *chips*).

Croc: Crocodile (see also *freshie* and *saltie*).

> *"She's been a little wobbly since the croc was shot. She says your friend did it."*
> The Family Made of Dust

For more information, see *Amazing Australia*.

Crocodile Dundee: A character in a worldwide hit film based on the true exploits of Rodney Ansell, who survived being stranded in the *outback* for fifty-six days.

> *"All you Yanks think we're Crocodile Dundee out here, wrestling crocodiles and running around in the bush!"*
> Woman Alone

Crook: To be ill; to be broken.

Crooked on: To be angry about (something).

Crow eater: Someone from South Australia, an arid area with an abundance of crows and ravens.

Crumblies: Elderly parents; from *Violet Crumble*.

Crystal fire: A type of opal that shows various colors, usually red, blue and green, mostly mined in *Coober Pedy*.

> *Lustrous bars of lime and candied apple sparkled in the crystal fire opal.*
> Woman Alone

Cunnamulla cartwheel: Wide-brimmed hat.

Cuppa: Cup of tea.

Cut lunch: A sandwich.

D

Dag: A clown or goofball; excrement stuck to wool on a sheep's rear; term of endearment.
Daggy: Loutish.
Dairy: Quickie mart or corner shop (see also *milk bar*).
Daks: Pants.
Damper: Unleavened bread; one of the main staples of the *Outback*.

> He dug damper, a type of unleavened bread, fresh from the pit oven. After he had sawed off the burned crust, the sweet, thick slices were dressed with melted butter.
> Woman Alone

Damp squib: Dull-witted (see *squib*).
Dandaraga: (Aboriginal.) Fertile land.
Dark on: To be angry about (something).
Darling pea: A type of legume, the Swainsona, that causes twitching, odd posture, and other strange behavior in animals that graze on it. Although deadly, the plant is also addictive.
  For more information, see *Amazing Australia*.
Darling shower: *Dust storm*; term originated in the Darling area.
Darts: The game of darts, which can be found in nearly every *pub*.

> In the corner, a young woman played darts as surreptitiously as possible.
> Woman Alone

Darwin stubbie: A bottle of beer that holds over a liter of alcohol (see *stubbie*).
Dead horse: Catsup (see *sauce*).
Dead marine: Empty beer bottle.
Death adder: One of the deadliest snakes in Australia and the world.

> Death adders felt at home with possums in the rainforest while cockatoos hung out with koalas in eucalyptus groves. Territories meant little and boundaries didn't exist.
> Seven Sisters

  For more information, see *Amazing Australia*.
Deep sinker: Tall beer glass.
Derribong: (Aboriginal.) Green trees.

Desal: Desalinated water, used frequently along the western coast of Australia.

> *Whenever I chanced upon fresh water, usually from supplies hauled to the roadhouses by tankers, I topped off my containers. The fresh was reserved for drinking and the desal served for washing... My clothes degenerated from hopeless to laughable. At least everything matched.*
> Woman Alone

Devils Marbles: Also (Aboriginal) Karlu Karlu, Devils Marbles Conservation Reserve. A site, consisting of scattered boulders, of deep spiritual significance to the Aboriginal owners. The English name refers to John Ross' comment made during his expedition to lay out the telegraph line: "This is the Devil's country; he's even emptied his bag of marbles around the place!"

> *At a tourist site called Devil's Marbles, a vendor remembered the odd pair and pointed to a faint track heading west.*
> The Family Made of Dust

For more information, see *18,000 Miles*.

Dial: Face; derived from a watch's face.

Dicky: Uncertain, risky.

Didgeridoo: American spelling of the word used for an Aboriginal wind instrument (see *didjeridoo*).

> *He played the didgeridoo while she danced.*
> Seven Sisters

Didjeridoo: Traditional Aboriginal wind instrument, the sound of which is often compared to a foghorn.

> *Kinks and curves enhanced the richness of the sound, and the best didgeridoos had a flare at the bottom that could disperse the sound.*
> Woman Alone

Digger: Aussie soldier.

Dill: Idiot.

Dilly: Silly, absentminded.

Dilly bag: Small bag for carrying food or miscellaneous items.

> *In his dilly bag, a pouch sewn from kangaroo hide, were bits of food the men had handled.*
> The Family Made of Dust

Dingbat: Idiot; eccentric person.

Dingbats: Delirium tremens or DTs, the confusion caused by alcohol withdrawal.

Dingo: A wild dog native to Australia; also a cunning person, derived from the wild dog's reputation as an animal that slinks unseen through the _bush_ before attacking.

Dingoes drooled at the thought of slaking their thirst with blood.
Seven Sisters

For more information, see *Amazing Australia.*

Dingo fence: A fence that runs across thousands of kilometers from the eastern coast to the southern coast to protect sheep from predation by _dingoes_ (see also _rabbit fence_).

A solo day trip took me to the dingo fence. The barrier began in Surfers' Paradise, Queensland and didn't stop until it hit the Great Australian Bight near Western Australia. That's 5,600 kilometers of wooden posts and wire stretched between the horizons.
Woman Alone

For more information, see *18,000 Miles.*

Dinkum, fair dinkum: True, honest, real.

Dinkum oil: Good information or lead (see _good oil, dinkum_).

Dinky-di: The real thing.

Dirt bike: A motorcycle fit for use on rugged terrain; used by modern Australian ranchers to _muster_ their animals.

Dirty on: To be annoyed with (something).

Dishlicker: Dog.

Divvy van: Police van.

Djang: (Aboriginal.) Spiritual energy, such as the energy arising from the _Dreamtime_.

Where the creators made camp, a sacred energy called djang *pooled in the earth. In these places men initiated boys and women bore children.*
The Family Made of Dust

Do a flit, do a moonlight flit: To leave unexpectedly in order to avoid responsibility.

Do a Melba: To repeatedly emerge from retirement.

Do a nickywoop: To leave quickly.

Do a perish: To be very hungry or thirsty (to die from hunger/thirst).

Dob: To tell stories about (someone); also a name or a nickname.

> *I had created what I considered to be a fairly large blaze when Dob, a leather-faced, wrinkle-eyed, gruff-and-grumble Aussie, clomped up. "Where's the fire?" he bellowed. "You call that a fire? I'll show you a fire!"*
> Woman Alone

Docket: Bill or receipt.

Doctor: Breeze that blows over Western Australia's coast off the Indian Ocean.

Do-dar: Thingamajig.

Dodgy: Suspicious or underhanded.

Doesn't know if he/she's Arthur or Martha: To be confused.

Doesn't know if it's Pitt Street or Christmas: To be confused. Refers to a *bushie* confused by the lights on Sydney's main downtown shopping drag.

Dog and bone: Telephone.

Doggo: Hidden.

Dog's breakfast: Chaotic.

Dog stiffener: Government-paid dingo culler (see *roo shooter*).

Done like dinner: Defeated; finished.

Done up like a pet lizard: Well-dressed.

Donger: Penis.

Don't give a stuff: Don't care.

Dosh: Money.

Dot-dot: Also dot painting. A technique (and the final product) where a series of small colored dots are painted onto canvas, wood, bark, or objects to create an Aboriginal painting that tells a story. Derived in the 1970s from traditional sand and body painting techniques.

Double-fronted: Duplex or split home.

Down the gurgler: Down the toilet; to go bad.

Down Under: Australia.

For more information, see *18,000 Miles.*

Do your block: To lose your temper.

Do your dash: To reach your limit.

Do your lolly: Throw a temper tantrum; to lose your temper.

Dragging the chain: To lag behind other drinkers, from a shearer's term meaning to lag behind.

Draw the crabs: To attract unwanted attention.

Dreaming: A *Dreamtime* story; also the sacred energy of the Dreamtime.

> *Animals and birds are connected by the energy*
> *of creation, by the Dreaming.*
> Seven Sisters

Dreaming Law: Sacred Aboriginal law based on ancient traditions and beliefs.

> *"Is that part of the Dreaming law?"*
> *"It's karma!" She laughed, the same breathless chime he had first*
> *heard under the coolibah tree at her house.*
> The Family Made of Dust

Dreaming site: A place that holds a specific *Dreamtime* tale.

> *The sorcerer left but not before looting the*
> *Dreaming sites of Yancy's tribe.*
> The Family Made of Dust

Dreamtime: The time of creation during which all the world and its living beings were formed. The *dreaming* continues today.

> *We truly are connected in the web of life, in*
> *this continuous Dreamtime.*
> Seven Sisters

Drink with the flies: To drink alone; to be unsociable.

Drippy: Boring.

Drive uphill with the clutch slipping: Stupid, dull-witted.

Drongo: Idiot; stupid person.

Drop a clanger: To make a social error.

Drop bear: A *koala*; derived from a joke Aussies like to pull on tourists.

> *For all I know, he still searches the trees for those*
> *elusive yet deadly drop bears.*
> Woman Alone

Drop in: To steal another surfer's wave.

Drop kick: Nasty or unlikeable person.

Drop off: (Imperative.) Go away.

Drop your bundle: To drop the ball, to let something slip; to give up.

Drop your guts: To fart.

Drover: Herdsman.

> *Bea's other son Rob used a dirt bike, the modern drover's mount, to cruise through the pasture until he located the animal.*
> Woman Alone

Drover's dog: An untrustworthy person; a person of no importance; useless.

Dry: The season during which little or no rain falls throughout much of Australia.

> *Each dry season the ground was brittle and ember-hot as they carried corpses to the tree.*
> The Family Made of Dust

For more information, see *18,000 Miles*.

Dry as a dead dingo's donger: Very dry.

Dry as a Pommie's towel: Thirsty; derogatory implications based on the stereotype that British people don't like to bathe (see *Pom, Pommie*).

Dry season: The long period of time during which little rain falls. (Also see *wet season*.)

Dubbo: Idiot.

Ducks and drakes: DTs, or delirium tremens, the shaking caused by alcohol withdrawal. Derived from rhyming slang (shakes).

Duck's dinner: A drink without anything to eat (see also *emu's breakfast*).

Duck's disease: Short legs.

Duckshoving: Cutting in line; underhanded business.

Duffer: Fool (teasing term rather than derogatory).

Dugout: A house dug out of the ground, frequently found in Coober Pedy.

> *Lots of people in Coober Pedy lived underground in dugouts, spaces they had carved out of the rock.*
> Woman Alone

For more information, see *18,000 Miles*.

Dunga: Angry.

Dunny: Outdoor toilet with or without flush capabilities.

For more information, see *18,000 Miles*.

Dunny brush: Crewcut (see *dunny*).

Dunny budgie: Fly (see *dunny*).

Durry: Cigarette.

Dust storm: Plumes of dust carried on the wind that can be measured in thousands of tons of dirt.

E

Eagle: Also wedge-tailed eagle, bunjil, eaglehawk. Australia's largest bird of prey. Often seen eating carrion on the highway.

> *As he stood there, an eagle struck him hard from behind.*
> *A sharp pain flared in his mind. His neck had been*
> *broken and he tumbled off the plateau.*
> Seven Sisters

For more information, see *Amazing Australia*.

Earbash: Nonstop chatter.

Earbasher: One who talks nonstop.

Earwig: Eavesdropper; to eavesdrop.

Eastern brown: The eastern *brown snake*.

> *Rachel had killed a snake for her meal, a python*
> *with the colors of an Eastern brown.*
> The Family Made of Dust

For more information, see *Amazing Australia*.

Easy as spearing an eel with a spoon: Difficult.

Echidna: Also *spiny echidna*. One of only four surviving monotremes, egg-laying mammals.

> *Echidnas and bats said that no secrets hid underground, and*
> *galahs who nested in hollow tree trunks couldn't*
> *claim any special knowledge.*
> Seven Sisters

For more information, see *Amazing Australia*.

Elder: An individual who has received a high level of respect in traditional Aboriginal culture.

> *Eventually the elder raised one hand. The bus dipped wildly*
> *as the driver stomped on the brakes.*
> Woman Alone

Elder council: A group of *elders* responsible for guiding an Aboriginal community.

> *In ancient times, the elder council eased the tension.*
> Seven Sisters

Elephant's, elephant's trunk: Drunk.

Emu: Australia's largest native bird, a flightless ratite with soft, brown feathers.

> *I was much like that emu mother. I was in my late twenties and had turned down two marriage proposals already.*
> Woman Alone

For more information, see *Amazing Australia*.

Emu fat: The fat of the *emu* has long been used for its health properties by Aboriginal people; the oil is now available on the open market.

> *The sides had been rubbed with emu fat and decorated with red ochre and charcoal.*
> The Family Made of Dust

For more information and uses, see *Fairy Bread and Bush Tucker*.

Emu's breakfast: A drink and a good look around (see also *duck's dinner*).

Enzed: New Zealand; derived from the pronunciation of the acronym NZ.

Esky: Cooler; from popular brand name.

Eucalyptus forest: The iconic Australian forest, which includes roughly 900 species of trees.

> *Past the Carrara Range, the eucalyptus forests faded into plains dominated by mouse and hawk.*
> The Family Made of Dust

For more information, see *Amazing Australia*.

Every bastard and his dog: Everyone.

Evo: Evening.

Explosives: Homemade dynamite used in Coober Pedy by independent miners digging for opal.

> *"If you go to the drive-in theater, there's a sign at the entrance that reads* No Explosives. *Bloody idiots drink too much and smoke in their cars."*
> Woman Alone

F

Face like a chook's ass/a yard of tripe: Sad expression (see *chook*).
Face like the bottom of a capsicum: Sour or sad expression (see *capsicum*).
Fair cow: Disagreeable.
Fair crack of the whip: A fair chance.
Fair dinkum: Genuine, honest, at the core of an issue (see *dinkum*).
Fair enough: Expression of agreement; expression to concede that the speaker is correct.

> *"Just say the word and I'll shut this fella up fast."*
> *"Fair enough. But at the right time and in the right way."*
> The Family Made of Dust

Fair go: An opportunity, a good chance.
Fair suck of the sauce: A fair chance (see *sauce*).
Fang doctor, fang carpenter: Dentist.
Fanny: Female genitalia. This particular slang word causes a lot of amusement when American tourists talk about their fanny packs.
Far gone: To be in love; drunk.
Female dreaming: *Songs*, stories and *Dreamtime* energy that deals with *women's business*.
Feral cat: A cat originally domesticated or one that descended from a domesticated lineage that lives in the wild.

> *He stared out the window as if he could conjure the past. He saw only the imported rabbits that stole the grass, the feral cats that decimated native species.*
> The Family Made of Dust

For more information, see *Amazing Australia*.
Few stubbies short of a six-pack: Stupid (see *stubby*).
Finger talk: Sign language used to communicate with members of tribes that use dissimilar languages; also used during hunting to maintain silence.

> *When they cut him down, half conscious and bloated with welts, his hands signaled defiantly. He cursed them with finger talk, the silent language of the hunt.*
> The Family Made of Dust

Fit as a Mallee bull: Healthy.
Fitz: A large sausage used for cold-cuts.

Fizzer: Something that does not live up to expectations.
Flake: Shark meat; generic fish-n-chips shop fillets.
Flaked out: To be tired; passed out.
Flaming: Curse, used as an adjective.
Flaming good time: Exceptionally good time.
Flash: Great; well-dressed.
Flat chat: Speaking very quickly.
Flat out: To do something very quickly, frantically, or nonstop.
Flat to the boards: To be or to act frantic.
Flinders grass: Several types of pasture grass that can grow up to forty inches tall.
   For more information, see *Amazing Australia*.
Floater: A *meat pie* tucked into a bowl of pea soup.
Flog the cat: To pity yourself.
Flounder spearer: Conductor.
Flush toilet: A toilet that uses water to flush away waste; differentiated from a pit toilet.

> *A long pause in the Blue Mountains allowed me to become acquainted with the camping lifestyle without missing out on showers or flush toilets.*
> Woman Alone

Flutter: A bet.
Flyer: Female grey kangaroo (see also *boomer*).
   For more information, see *Amazing Australia*.
Flying fox: A fruit-eating bat that looks very much like a tiny fox with wings.

> *Owl was a crafty fellow. He said that if they didn't fight, they would be considered traitors. And since Flying Fox was related to both sides, she couldn't risk joining whichever side would eventually lose.*
> Seven Sisters

   For more information, see *Amazing Australia*.
Flywire: Window screen.
(like) Flywire on a submarine: Useless (see *flywire*).
Footbrawl: Disparaging term for *footy*.
Footpath: Sidewalk.
Footy: Australian rules football.
For fun and fancy to please old Nancy: For no particular reason.
Fossicking: Searching for fossils, precious metals or gemstones.

Freshie: A freshwater crocodile (see also *croc, saltie*).

Frilled lizard: Also frilled-neck lizard, frilled dragon, frilled agama. A species of lizard in Australia and New Guinea with a large ruff supported by spines it displays when threatened. Also a bearded man.

For more information, see *Amazing Australia*.

Frock: Woman's dress.

Front: To confront (someone).

Full as a boot, full as a goog: Drunk; stuffed (see *goog*).

Full as a phone book: Drunk; stuffed.

Full feather: In good health.

Full quid: Intelligent; sharp in business (see *quid*).

Further back than Walla-Walla: Behind schedule; last (see *Walla-Walla*).

G

Galah: Also (Aboriginal) gilaa. A small *cockatoo* with a grey back and pink belly; also a silly fool or idiot, derived from the bird's behavior.

> *At the southernmost point of the wetlands, the birds gathered their own forces. Cranes and herons stood as thick as river reeds. Flocks of galahs thousands strong wheeled overhead.*
> Seven Sisters

For more information, see *Amazing Australia*.

Game: Brave; foolhardy.

Game as a piss ant: Very daring, particularly said of a short person.

Garbo: Garbage man.

Gas: Propane (see also *petrol, autogas*).

> *Adding to the child's comfort were folding tables, throne-like folding chairs, portable two- and four-burner stoves, five-gallon cook pots, a gas-powered mini refrigerator, an entire box of spices, wash buckets and gas lampposts, folding cots with mattresses, and plenty of blankets that surely weren't soggy.*
> Woman Alone

For more information, see *18,000 Miles*.

G'day: General greeting; short for "good day to you."

Gee and tee: Gin and tonic.

Geebung: Settler.

Get a leg up: To start; to have help getting something started.

Get knotted: (Imperative.) Go to hell.

Get off your bike: To become angry.

Get on your goat: To become irritated.

Get the Guernsey: To be recognized for some special action or trait.

Get up my nose: To pester or irritate (someone).

Gew-gaw: Gaudy, tacky.

Ghost gum: A type of Corymbia tree with a smooth, white bark that glows in the moonlight.

> *Ghost gums rushed up to the road, their branches a caterwaul of scratches.*
> The Family Made of Dust

For more information, see *Amazing Australia*.

Gibber: A large rock; a desert.

For more information, see *18,000 Miles*.

Gink: A clown or joker.

Girl's home: An orphanage that shelters girls; holds a negative connotation due to their widespread use with the *Stolen Generations*.

> "Him tell my great-granny's death, just before I were put in a girl's home. Weren't much of a girl after that. Grow up quick in them homes."
> The Family Made of Dust

Girramay: An Aboriginal tribe in Queensland.

> *This part of the Kirrama Range traditionally belonged to the Girramay people and was loaded with waterfalls.*
> Woman Alone

Git: A foolish or annoying person.

> "Like taking your date to the theater and some git tells her she shouldn't have half-caste children because they'll be disadvantaged."
> The Family Made of Dust

Give a bell: To call someone on the telephone.

Give a curry: To tease.

Give it a go/a bur/a bash: To try something.

Give it away: To give up.

Give it the flick: To discard (something).

Give (someone) the irrits/the pip: To irritate (someone).

Goanna: Monitor lizard; piano. Latter usage derived from the exceptional length of the monitor lizard, which could cover a piano's keyboard.

> *The bloated carcass of a goanna, the boy's favorite kind of meat, lay beside her.*
> Seven Sisters

For more information, see *Amazing Australia*.

For recipes, see *Fairy Bread and Bush Tucker*.

Gob: Mouth.

Go crook: To become angry.

God botherer: Religious fanatic.

Go down the gurgler: To go bad; to go down the drain.

Go down with the rain: To fail or disappear, as rainwater falls and then swirls away.

> *Melody had been a teacher and a health counselor for the local tribes until her job had "gone down with the rain."*
> Woman Alone

Godzone: New Zealand (from *God's own*).

Go to hospital: To go to the hospital; to see the doctor.

Golliwog: A racially offensive mascot used by a certain brand of marmalade in the mid- to late twentieth century.

> *It had been his curse that his favorite brand of marmalade had a coal-faced, kinky haired mascot known as the Golliwog.*
> The Family Made of Dust

Go mulga: To travel into the *Outback* (see *mulga*).

Good-o: Exclamation of agreement.

Good oil: Useful information; the truth (see *dinkum oil*).

Good on ya: Congratulatory term; "Good for you!"

Goog: Egg.

Goondiwindi: (Aboriginal.) Water running over rocks.

For more information, see *18,000 Miles*.

Gordonvale: A small town in the Cairns Region of Queensland.

For more information, see *18,000 Miles*.

Got a license from a Wheatie's packet: Incompetent driver or practitioner.

Go to buggery: (Imperative.) Go away.

Go to market: To become angry.

Got the Darling pea: To behave strangely (see *Darling pea*).

Go twenty to the dozen: To do (something) quickly.

Grave jumper: Someone who takes over another's position or office too quickly after the person has left.

Grazier: Sheep or cattle farmer.

Greaser: One who uses flattery.

Great Australian adjective: Bloody hell.

Great Australian Bight: A large bay off the southern coast.

For more information, see *18,000 Miles*.

Great Divide: A mountain range west of Sydney, NSW.

For more information, see *18,000 Miles*.

Green ant: Also weaver ant. An aggressively defensive arboreal ant that builds nests by weaving together leaves.

> *A squadron of green ants, knocked from their tree by the rain,*
> *stood guard on the crossbeams of the tent.*
> Woman Alone

For more information, see *Amazing Australia*.

Grevillea shrub: A diverse genus of flowering plants native to rainforests and open habitats.

> *To their right a thicket of grevillea shrubs*
> *blazed with golden flowers.*
> The Family Made of Dust

For more information, see *Amazing Australia*.

Grill: A barbeque that often has a griddle-style cooking surface rather than a grill (see also *barbie*).

Grinding rock: A rock used to grind the seeds of native plants into flour.

> *He heard the patter of the millet atop the grinding rock and the*
> *splash of dirt pitched from the coolamon.*
> Seven Sisters

Grog: Usually applies to beer but can indicate any alcoholic substance.

> *He watched as the white thug sank into his grog.*
> The Family Made of Dust

Grommet: Surfer known for tricks or antics.

Grong Grong: (Aboriginal.) Very hot. Instead of using a modifier like "very," many tribal languages simply repeat the word to provide emphasis.

Grotty: Dirty; untidy; secondhand.

Ground parrot: Small farmer (see *cockie*).

Grouse: Great, terrific; to complain.

Grub: Child; food.

Grunter: A wild pig.

> *Ben must have been especially brave to duck through*
> *shrubs where the grunters hid.*
> Woman Alone

For more information, see *Amazing Australia*.

For recipes, see *Fairy Bread and Bush Tucker*.

Gub, gubbah: (Aboriginal.) A Caucasian. Can be used in a derogatory way.

Guest house: Private *hotel* that serves breakfast as part of the room rate (see also *pub*).

For more information, see *18,000 Miles*.

Guff off: To be lazy.
Gum, gumtree: Eucalypt tree.

> *A network of creeks and rivers that ran only during the Wet sustained gum trees taller than most buildings.*
> The Family Made of Dust

For more information, see *Amazing Australia*.

Gumbies, gum boots: Pull-on boots with rubber soles popular in the *Outback*.

Gunyah: (Aboriginal.) Shelter made of brush constructed so that it sheds water.

> *Whenever he appeared, all the ladies hid in their gunyahs....*
> Seven Sisters

Gutzer: A plan that fails.

H

Haboob: A *dust storm* frequently associated with cold fronts, especially in Central Australia.

For more information, see *18,000 Miles.*

Hair like a bush pig's ass: Disheveled hair.

Hairstring: Twine spun from human hair and plant fiber or animal fur.

> *Dana heard the feathery scream rise from her dreams and adjusted the hairstring around her torso.*
> The Family Made of Dust

Half your luck: (As in, "I'd like to have....") Fantastic luck.

Hang on a tick: (Imperative.) Wait a second.

Hare-wallaby: One of several types of marsupials that look a bit like rabbits, or hares (see *wallaby*).

For more information, see *Amazing Australia.*

Hare-wallaby men: A clan of the *Pitjantjatjara* tribe.

> *Long ago, their stories said, the Hare-wallaby men gathered for a ceremony.*
> The Family Made of Dust

Has a death adder in the pocket: Cheap person.

Hasn't got a bean/cracker: Broke.

Hasn't got all four paws on the mouse: Stupid.

Hatter: Loner.

Have a yarn: To talk to someone.

Have to run around in the shower to get wet: Said of someone who is thin.

Head like a mini with the doors open: Said of someone who has protruding ears.

Head like a robber's dog: Ugly.

Head starter: First drink of the day.

Heaps: Plenty; tons (of something).

> *"This hotel is his, and while they were excavating, he pulled heaps of opal from the ground."*
> Woman Alone

Hey: What? Or, pardon me? Also used to prompt a response.

> *"How do you like mining, then?" Marie asked over dinner. "Dirty work, hey?"*
> Woman Alone

High as a dingo's howl: An unbearably foul smell.

Hit your kick: To spend money.

Holiday: A personal vacation.

> *The occupants, a young couple on holiday, honored me with more than one glance.*
> Woman Alone

Homestead: A ranch; also the original or primary (owner's) house built on the ranch.

> *And so began the tallying of trucks and tractors, the price the homestead would fetch at auction, the money Rita had stashed in a tin.*
> The Family Made of Dust

Honey ant: Also honeypot ant. A type of ant that stores liquid nourishment, often nectar, in the abdominal cavities of select members.

> *"Honey ants," she said. "They're sweet. Want to try one?"*
> Woman Alone

For more information, see *Amazing Australia*.

For recipes, see *Fairy Bread and Bush Tucker*.

Hoon: A showoff; a loudmouth.

Horsefly: True flies, the females of which bite to obtain blood.

> *The bushflies squeezed through the weave, leaving their larger horsefly cousins despondently attached to the exterior.*
> Woman Alone

For more information, see *Amazing Australia*.

Hotel: A pub that might rent rooms. Australian liquor laws used to ban the sale of alcohol past 6 p.m. When an exception was made for establishments that rented rooms, many pubs began renting rooms.

> *Despite the hotel's upscale atmosphere, the pub was the dim, smoky enclave Australians craved.*
> The Family Made of Dust

For more information, see *18,000 Miles*.

Hottie: Hot water bottle.

How long is a piece of string: Retort that indicates the question has no answer.

Hump, speed hump: Speed bump.

Humpy: Rural house that has been thrown together.

Hunting boomerang: A non-returning boomerang with one leg shorter than the other. Used to stun prey or break an animal's bones.

He carved four giant boomerangs, the kind that didn't return, then painted them white on top and black on the bottom.
Seven Sisters

I

I could eat a horse and chase the jockey: An expression meaning *I'm very hungry.*

Icy pole: Popsicle.

Illawarra: (Aboriginal.) A coastal region in New South Wales; name means "high place by the sea."

For more information, see *18,000 Miles.*

Iltilpa: (Aboriginal.) A type of *grevillea* commonly called beefwood; also the grub that feeds on the tree.

Dana would throw the hairs of iltilpa,
the itchy grub, into his mouth.
The Family Made of Dust

In a divvy: Pregnant.

In a shit, shitty: In a foul mood.

In donkey's years: A long time.

In good nick: In good shape; all right.

In the cactus: In trouble.

In the nick: Naked; in jail.

In the nuddy: Naked.

In the shits: In trouble.

In your boot: Exclamation indicating disagreement.

Iparrpe: (Aboriginal.) Meaning "quick" in the *Arrernte* language.

"Run here!" Andy cried. "Iparrpe, quickly!" Their cousin
was already gone, hidden by scrub or running
low through a dry creek bed.
The Family Made of Dust

Ironwood: Type of Casuarina trees known for having exceptionally strong wood.

He selected his best club, the one made of
ironwood, and tied it to his belt.
Seven Sisters

For more information, see *Amazing Australia.*

Irrwerlenge: (Aboriginal; Arrernte language.) A type of *grevillea* with golden flowers.

"That's Selena's totem," he said. "It's called irrwerlenge.*"*
The Family Made of Dust.

For more information, see *Amazing Australia.*

Itchy grub: Processionary caterpillars, the hairs of which can cause skin rashes and swelling.

For more information, see *Amazing Australia.*

It pivots on: It depends on.

It's a goer: It is definite.

J

Jabiru: A type of stork found in Australia's northern region.

> *In other areas, Kakadu was lush. I trod a marsh that catered to the magnificent jabiru, a black-necked stork.*
> Woman Alone

Jack: To be tired of or bored with (something).
Jack and Jill: Bill, invoice.
Jackaroo/jillaroo: Ranch hand.

> *Not even teenagers looking to try the jackaroo lifestyle smiled so generously.*
> The Family Made of Dust

Jack in the box: Nervous or twitchy person.
Jack up: To refuse to do what you're told.
Jaffle: Toasted sandwich.
Jake: Good, all right.
Jam cake: A pastry made with fruit jam as the filling.

> *The group had stopped in a clearing to make tea and nibble on jam cakes.*
> Woman Alone

For more information and recipes, see *Fairy Bread and Bush Tucker*.

Jam roll: A thin layer of cake spread with jam and rolled up before being sliced.

> *Within minutes the tea was ready, the bush tucker was passed around on pieces of bark, and jam rolls satisfied timid palates.*
> Woman Alone

For more information and recipes, see *Fairy Bread and Bush Tucker*.

Jarrah jerker: Lumberjack.
Jigged: Broken.
Jiggered: Broken; useless.
Jimjams: Anxious feeling.
Joe Bloggs: Joe Blow, the average person.
Joey: Baby kangaroo.

For more information, see *Amazing Australia*.

Jolly: Very.

Journo: Journalist.

Judder bars: Speed bumps.

Jumbuck: Sheep.

For more information, see *Amazing Australia*.

Jumper: Sweater.

Just down the road: Might be fifty yards, might be fifty miles. The enormous empty tracts between towns have given Aussies a strange perception of distance.

K

Kafuffle: Disturbance.

Kakadu: A large national park in the Northern Territory. Name derived from a misspelling of Gaagudju, the name of the Aboriginal language spoken in the area.

> *Piebald geese were satisfied with Kakadu's marshlands and scrub turkeys darted into the jungles.*
> Seven Sisters

For more information, see *18,000 Miles.*

Kangaroo: One of many marsupials from the Macropodidae family native to Australia.

> *He peered at me as if I might be joking. To him, kangaroos were dogfood.*
> Woman Alone

For more information, see *Amazing Australia.*

For recipes, see *Fairy Bread and Bush Tucker.*

Kapok: A tree that produces a seed pod filled with cottony fluff.

> *The youngest sister, a reed-thin girl with hair like the floss of a kapok tree, began to cry.*
> Seven Sisters

For more information, see *Amazing Australia.*

Karadji: Also *clever man*. A ritual executioner sent by the *elder council* to dispense punishment.

> *"These belonged to a karadji man, the fellow responsible for enforcing punishments handed down by the elders. If an Aboriginal women saw these she'd probably run away screaming."*
> Woman Alone

Karratha: A city in Western Australia's Pilbara region.

> *As dusk fell at Karratha, a family invited me to join them at their picnic table. The mother broke out a bag of potato chips while I loaded the kids with pastry.*
> Woman Alone

For more information, see *18,000 Miles.*

Keen as mustard: Enthusiastic.

Kiddiewink: Child.

Killing: The slaughter of livestock; also the execution of a criminal by a _karadji_.

> "They reckon you're a little weird," he said, "taking
> pictures of the killing and all."
> Woman Alone

(the) Killing Time: Also Killing Times. The period of rapid expansion by settlers during which Aboriginal people were massacred by being hunted down or by being given food that had been poisoned.

> It was the Killing Time, a twenty-year period when retribution
> parties rode out like the monstrous Dreamtime cannibals.
> The Family Made of Dust

(the) Kimberley: Also Kimberley region. The northernmost region in Western Australia. Contains a number of unique geological sites and is the source for _Kimberley pink_ diamonds.

> "I'm taking the family through the Kimberley," he said, "and
> around the Top End. I'm about to sell the truck and want
> the children to have a real bush experience first."
> Woman Alone

For more information, see _18,000 Miles_.

Kimberley pink: A type of diamond ranging from intense purplish-pink to Champaign pink; sourced only from the _Kimberley_.

> Gabe opened his eyes to air the misty pink of Kimberley diamonds.
> The Family Made of Dust

For more information, see _18,000 Miles_.

King snake: Also king brown, mulga snake, Pilbara cobra. One of the longest snakes in Australia; despite its name, it is in the black snake genus.

> He slid through the gloom like a king snake through spinifex.
> The Family Made of Dust

For more information, see _Amazing Australia_.

Kip: Nap.

Kiwi: Someone from New Zealand; named for the flightless bird indigenous to New Zealand.

Knackers: Testicles.

Knickers: Panties.

> *Rob wrestled a long bundle into the room and shut the door. "I rescued a bit more than your knickers."*
> The Family Made of Dust

Knock shop: Whorehouse.

Knock (someone) back: To turn down a proposition (for sex).

Koala: A marsupial native to Australia that lives in trees; the koala climbs down only on the rare occasions when it needs to drink.

> *Whenever koala's descendants are hunted for food, their bones are never broken to honor the orphan's ability to survive the harsh punishment.*
> Seven Sisters

For more information, see *Amazing Australia*.

Kookaburra: A type of kingfisher native to Australia and New Guinea. Known for their raucous, laughing call.

> *A blue-winged kookaburra skimmed the pool, dipping its head to catch dribbles of water on its back before roosting on the fence.*
> Woman Alone

For more information, see *Amazing Australia*.

Koori: (Aboriginal.) From the Awabakal language. A tribal people in Newcastle.

> *Artifacts from other tribes—the Pintupi of the Western Desert, the Yirrkala along the north coast, the Koori in the south—were fair game.*
> The Family Made of Dust

Kriol: An *Australian creole*, a stable and natural language that developed when English was mixed with tribal languages (see also *pidgin*).

Kulpunya: (Aboriginal.) A *dingo*, also a *Dreamtime* dog formed from sticks and other items. From the *Pitjantjatjara* tribe.

> *By day songs filled Kulpunya with evil and by night the creature took form.*
> The Family Made of Dust

Kumoken: (Aboriginal.) Freshwater crocodile. From a tribe in Western Arnhem Land, Northern Territory.

> *"Kumoken big snapper, got big power."*
> The Family Made of Dust

Kurrajong: The bottlebrush tree or shrub.

They were the same golden yellow as the hairs on kurrajong seeds, the lilac of the flowers tucked into headbands during dances.
The Family Made of Dust

For more information, see *Amazing Australia*.

L

Lady blamey: A glass fashioned from the bottom half of a beer bottle.

Lady finger: Miniature banana.

    For more information and recipes, see *Fairy Bread and Bush Tucker*.

Lady muck: Stuck-up woman.

Lady's waist: Beer glass nipped in at the middle.

Lag: To inform on (someone).

Lair: One who is dressed up.

Lair up: To dress up.

Lamington: Sponge cake coated with various flavors of icing, usually chocolate; can be filled with jelly, cream, or both.

    For more information and recipes, see *Fairy Bread and Bush Tucker*.

Land claim: A parcel of land ceded back to the Aboriginal people whose ancestors lived there before settlers arrived.

> *Eventually the places where Aboriginal people lived evolved into land claims.*
> Woman Alone

    For more information, see *18,000 Miles*.

Land rights: The rights of Aboriginal tribes to the land where they lived before settlers arrived.

> *Oh, they knew about the Aboriginal land rights issues that had consumed the media for decades, and had heard about the children adopted by white families in a long-defunct effort to assimilate the race.*
> The Family Made of Dust

    For more information, see *18,000 Miles*.

Larrikin: Clown, oaf.

Lash out: To spend wildly.

Laughing gear: Mouth.

Lav, lavvy: Toilet.

Law: Also *Dreaming* law. The mores and beliefs laid down by the *Dreamtime* stories.

> *According to traditional law, a man who was strong and capable might take more than one wife.*
> Seven Sisters

Layby: An area set aside by the government where travelers can camp for free.

> *At a layby ... outside Gordonvale, horses and cattle grazed near a raised railroad trestle.*
> Woman Alone

Lease: The land leased from the government by ranchers.
Lemon squash: Lemonade.
Lerp: An insect that sucks sap from plants or trees and creates honeydew.

> *"Any lerps in my teeth? Don't you hate it when you're talking to some bloke and he won't tell you there's a big green bug caught in your choppers?"*
> The Family Made of Dust

For more information on the insect, see *Amazing Australia*.
For information on food use, see *Fairy Bread and Bush Tucker*.
Liana: A type of vine found in the tropical and subtropical rainforest.

> *Their trunks were wreathed with liana vines that climbed toward the elusive sun.*
> Woman Alone

For more information, see *Amazing Australia*.
Lick: Feed set out for cattle.

> *"It rained a few days ago, so I have to tip out the barrels and load them with fresh lick."*
> Woman Alone

Lie doggo: To lay low (see _doggo_).
Lift: Elevator.
(like a) Lily on a dustbin: Forlorn; lonely.
Lippie: Lipstick.
Liquid amber: Beer.
Liquid laugh: Vomit.
Little Vegemite: Child (see also _Vegemite_).
(like a) Lizard drinking: Nonstop.

> *Ian's white Land Rover was nearly twenty years old and it still ran like a lizard drinking—nonstop and practically unstoppable.*
> The Family Made of Dust

Lob, lob in: To drop by for a visit.

Locust: A cicada, some of which can produce sounds as loud as 120 decibels.

For more information, see *Amazing Australia*.

Lolly: Candy.

Lolly water: Soda.

Lonely as a bandicoot on a burnt ridge: Forlorn.

> *"She looks like a bandicoot on a burnt ridge." Rob stepped around the Falcon to survey the damage.*
> The Family Made of Dust

Long paddock: Strip of grass between a road and a fence; utilized by stations during drought as a source of fresh feed.

Loo: Toilet.

Lorikeet: Small and medium-sized parrots that feed on nectar.

> *A network of creeks and rivers that ran only during the Wet sustained gum trees taller than most buildings. Cockatoos raised their young in the hollow trunks, and after a rain lorikeets gorged on the nectar in the blossoms.*
> The Family Made of Dust

For more information, see *Amazing Australia*.

Lorry: A truck.

Lousy: Bad; cheap.

Love magic: Aboriginal ceremonies performed to cause someone to fall in love or to enhance the feeling of love between two people.

> *He even traded with the desert tribes for ochre and painted his body with the symbols of love magic.*
> Seven Sisters

Lucky Country: Australia. A term that is used favorably despite originating in Donald Horne's book, *The Lucky Country,* in which Australia was viewed negatively.

Lunatic soup: Cheap wine (also see *plonk*).

M

Mad as a cut snake: Insanely angry.

Mad as a gumtree full of galahs: Crazy (see *galah*).

(like a) Mad woman's breakfast: Chaotic; in a state of disarray.

Magpie goose: A black and white water bird found in northern coastal Australia.

> *Magpie geese and ibis mingled with cranes that combed the marsh.*
> Woman Alone

For more information, see *Amazing Australia*.

Make a crust: To earn a living.

Make a proper galah: To embarrass one's self (see *galah*).

Make a quid: To earn a living (see *quid*).

Male dreaming: The ceremonies and songs associated with *men's business*.

> *The teen was fascinated, possibly even astonished. The djang in these rocks was male Dreaming.*
> The Family Made of Dust

Mallee: Shrub-like *eucalypt* trees; a stand of eucalypt trees.

> *My attention shifted to the basics: water for day and warmth for night. In the light the pure rain ran like cool satisfaction over my tongue, and in the dark the heat of sunbeams captured by spinifex and mallee bathed my skin.*
> Woman Alone

For more information, see *Amazing Australia*.

Man-making: Traditional Aboriginal ceremonies associated with a boy's coming-of-age.

> *When one boy failed the man-making ceremony, the shame was more than he could bear.*
> Seven Sisters

March flies: Biting flies that can cause a dangerous amount of blood loss in livestock when their numbers spike.

For more information, see *Amazing Australia*.

Marmite: The British or New Zealand version of *Vegemite*.

Mataranka: A small pastoral town in the Northern Territory.

> *"So you passed Mataranka? If you really thought someone was after you, why didn't you file a report there?"*
> The Family Made of Dust

For more information, see *18,000 Miles*.

Mate: Friend, pal.

> *The butcher smiled when the newcomer sat next to him. "Say, your best mate just left."*
> The Family Made of Dust

Mate's rates: Reduced prices for friends and relatives.

Matilda: Sleeping bag.

Me: My or mine; also used in the usual way to mean "myself."

> *"Maybe it's because you remind me of me dad."*
> The Family Made of Dust

Mean: Tightfisted.

Mean as bird shit: Very tightfisted.

Meat pie: Popular entree similar to potpie made with everything from steak to kidney and heart (see also *floater*).

For recipes, see *Fairy Bread and Bush Tucker*.

Meat sheet: A tarp or cloth laid down to protect freshly butchered meat.

> *As the quarters were lowered onto a meat sheet, an old linen spread across the bed of a truck, Kevin chased the dogs from the viscera.*
> Woman Alone

Men's business: The spiritual and ceremonial issues associated with an Aboriginal man's way of life.

> *Nowadays the chores, duties and ceremonies of men, called men's business, are less often separated from women's business.*
> Seven Sisters

Merino: Australian sheep breed that produces superior wool.

Message stick: A stick carved with notches used by Aboriginal tribes to send messages.

> *Gabe cradled the message stick. He had clung to this link,*
> *hoping it would lead to Ian. Now the artifact seemed*
> *translucent to everyone but him.*
> The Family Made of Dust

Metallic starling: Also shining starling. A starling native to Australia and Papua New Guinea that has glossy feathers and brilliant red eyes.

> *The blood was brilliant at first, like the eyes of the metallic*
> *starlings that congregated around his boyhood home.*
> The Family Made of Dust

For more information, see *Amazing Australia*.

Middy: Half a pint of beer ordered as a single serving.

Milk bar: Quickie mart or corner store (see *dairy*).

For more information, see *18,000 Miles*.

Milk train: A train that operates very early in the morning to deliver milk to remote towns; the same trains often carry passengers.

Mimi: Mythological spirits that Aboriginal tribes said could move through solid rock and fly.

> *A human form drawn like a stick figure was attributed to the*
> *Mimi, spirit people with supernatural powers.*
> Woman Alone

Mingy: Tightfisted.

Mintabie: (Place name.) An opal mining community in South Australia located on an Aboriginal *land claim*.

For more information, see *18,000 Miles*.

Miserable as a bandicoot: Very miserable (see *bandicoot*).

Missus: Wife.

> *Rob dropped his spoon into his bowl. "Right lovely stew,*
> *missus. Not even me mum could do better."*
> The Family Made of Dust

Mitchell grass: The genus Astrebla is the dominant grass throughout much of Australia's arid interior. Named after the Scottish explorer Thomas Mitchell.

For more information, see *Amazing Australia*.

Mittagong: (Place name.) Commonly known as Mitta. A town in New South Wales with many wineries. Name is said to come from an Aboriginal word meaning "little mountain."

> *Ragged paths led to Mittagong and Kaileroi and Undilla, sounds heavy with Aboriginal history.*
> The Family Made of Dust

For more information, see *18,000 Miles*.

Mob: Group of people or things; group of kangaroos.

> *When he spotted a mob of kangaroos grazing on a hilltop, he reached for the weapon.*
> Woman Alone

Moiety: The system governing kinship ties among Aboriginal tribes.

> *Love affairs that crossed moiety boundaries ... were contrary to the Dreaming law.*
> Seven Sisters

Mollydooker: Left-handed person.

Moosh: Mouth.

Mopoke: A bird that disguises itself during daylight by sitting very still; also a boring person, derived from the bird's daytime behavior.

For more information, see *Amazing Australia*.

More front than Myers: Forward; bold. Derived from Myers, a large department store with a long storefront.

Mouth like the bottom of cockie's cage: Dry mouth from a hangover (see *cockie*).

Mozzie: Mosquito.

For more information, see *Amazing Australia*.

Mperlkere: (Aboriginal.) *Arrernte* word for a Caucasian person.

> *This man was not the police, he knew, but he was mperlkere, white like the police. The children were supposed to run into the bush where the mperlkere couldn't see, where the mperlkere wouldn't go.*
> The Family Made of Dust

Muck about: To mess around, to play with.

Mulga: Shrub-like *acacia* trees; a stand of acacia.

> *Occasionally the town consisted of two or three shops but often they were lonely roadhouses dropped among the mulga.*
> Woman Alone

For more information, see *Amazing Australia*.

Mulga madness: Insanity or eccentric behavior brought on by living alone or in the *Outback*.

Mulga seed: The seeds of a *mulga* tree, which were used as a food source by Aboriginal tribes.

> *"My skin is lighter and my face isn't as broad but those people looked like me. My face, my head, my hands. And all they ever did was winnow mulga seed or eat ants or carve toys."*
> The Family Made of Dust

For more information and recipes, see *Fairy Bread and Bush Tucker*.

Mulga-seed clan: A clan of the *Pitjantjatjara* tribe.

> *But the Mulga-seed clan was jealous and tried to create a dingo using bones and the hair of women.*
> The Family Made of Dust

Mulga wire: Grapevine on which gossip is spread. Possibly derived from the use of mulga wood as telegraph poles.

Mullet: A type of coastal and occasionally freshwater fish that was a popular food source for Aboriginal tribes in the *Top End*.

> *Mullet heads were snapped back to indicate that their necks had been broken.*
> Woman Alone

Munga: (Aboriginal.) Food (also see *tucker*).

Murrumbidgee: (Aboriginal.) (Place name.) Large body of water.

Murrumbidgee jam: Brown sugar mixed with cold tea and spread on toast or *damper*.

Muster: To round up livestock.

> *"We normally only ride to muster cattle,"* Ben said.
> Woman Alone

Mutton: The meat from a mature sheep, as opposed to meat from a young lamb.

> *"Your cook served a man while I picked out this mutton,"* Rob said.
> The Family Made of Dust

For information and recipes, see *Fairy Bread and Bush Tucker*.

Mystery bag: Sausage.

For information and recipes, see *Fairy Bread and Bush Tucker*.

My stomach thinks my throat's cut: Expression meaning "I'm hungry."

N

Nacked: Angry; annoyed.

Nackered: Exhausted, worn out.

Namarakain: A certain type of spirit people who torment human beings; their fingers are joined with twine so they can trip people.

> *A shallow outcropping captured a Mimi-style battle sparked after a girl had been punished too severely. Superimposed atop this scene were the Namarakain, unearthly sisters who occasionally mutated into crocodiles and ate anyone who wandered by.*
> Woman Alone

Namarrkon: The spirit responsible for causing thunder and lightning.

> *Namarrkon the thunder spirit stood out due to his enormous eyes.*
> Woman Alone

Narked: Angry; irritated.

Narkie: Quick to anger.

Nasty piece of work: An unpleasant person.

National creed: Jokingly said to be: *If it moves, shoot it; if it doesn't, chop it down.*

Native bee: A stingless variety of tiny black bees.

> *The bush responded, sending brush-tailed possums to his window and stingless bees to build sugarbags in his favorite tree.*
> The Family Made of Dust

For more information, see *Amazing Australia*.

Native cherry: The fruit from a type of sandalwood that can be eaten raw or cooked; see also *bush cherry*.

For more information, see *Amazing Australia*.

For recipes, see *Fairy Bread and Bush Tucker*.

Native millet: Also Australian millet, papa grass, umbrella grass. The seeds from a species of native grass that used to be a staple food of Aboriginal tribes. Was also frequently used to make *damper*.

> *But native millet could be gathered easily from the ground and for now kept the tribe alive.*
> Seven Sisters

For more information, see *Amazing Australia*.

For recipes, see *Fairy Bread and Bush Tucker*.

Neddie: Horse.

Nelly: Cheap wine (see also *lunatic soup*, *plonk*).

Never Never: The Outback (see *Outback*).

New men: Boys who have returned to camp after their *man-making* ceremony; they are considered newly born and are therefore new men.

> *The boy sat alone on the plateau watching the new men being welcomed into the tribe.*
> Seven Sisters

New woman: A girl who has returned to camp after the ceremonies surrounding her first menses; she is considered newly born and is therefore a new woman.

New Zealand disease: To drown.

Ngathungi: Sticks that have been magically charmed to cause death; frequently used after a *bone pointing* has failed.

> *Then he coated the bundles with spinifex resin and set the* ngathungi *aside to cool.*
> The Family Made of Dust

Nick: Noun: a nickname. Verb: to steal.

Nicked: Stolen; arrested.

Nick off: To leave, particularly to leave in order to go into hiding.

Nick off: (Imperative.) Get lost, go away.

Nindalyup: (Aboriginal.) (Place name.) Crooked creek.

Nits in the network: Crazy.

No flies on: Intelligent, difficult to fool (someone).

No hoper: A total fool.

Nong: Idiot.

Noodle: To sift through mining slag looking for opal.

> *People who noodled the slag heaps could find a souvenir, unearth enough to cover their living expenses, or hit that one big chunk that would pay off their car.*
> Woman Alone

Not much chop: Not much good (see also *carry on like a pork chop*).

Not on your nellie: Exclamation indicating disagreement.

Not the full quid: Stupid, as in, "two bricks short of a full load" (see *quid*).

No worries: Expression meaning *no problem*.

> *"No worries! The sheilas like scars. Makes ya look*
> *like a spy or a secret military agent."*
> The Family Made of Dust

Ntaripe: (Aboriginal.) (Place name.) Heavitree Gap, a sacred *Dreaming* site that was "broken," or desecrated, when a gap was cut into the ridge to accommodate a roadway.

> *'Ntaripe, Heavitree Gap, was where the wild dogs fought."*
> The Family Made of Dust

For more information, see *18,000 Miles*.

Nulla nulla: (Aboriginal.) A fighting stick made from *blackbutt*, a hardwood.

> *A nulla nulla, a fighting stick ... was also used*
> *for digging or pounding food.*
> Woman Alone

Nut ducker: Person who avoids someone else.

O

Obiri Rock: A large rock formation in <u>Kakadu</u> National Park decorated with an especially thick collection of ancient art.

> *Obiri Rock, a deep overhang in the northeast corner of the park, had sheltered Aboriginal people during the wet.*
> Woman Alone

Ochre: A natural earth pigment that ranges from yellow through orange to red. Used in numerous Aboriginal ceremonies.

> *Rachel laid out her ochres and pulled a crystal from a shelf over her bed. She would have to work fast. She hoped it was not already too late.*
> The Family Made of Dust

Ocker: Australian redneck; an ignorant person.

Oenpelli: (Aboriginal.) (Place name.) An Aboriginal community, in the tribal language called Gunbalanya, on the eastern border of <u>Kakadu</u> National Park.

> *Neighbors came from as far as Oenpelli in the east and Victoria River to the south.*
> The Family Made of Dust

Of an evening: In the evening.

> *"You never went out of an evening," he shrugged. "You never saw him on his rounds."*
> The Family Made of Dust

Off: Spoiled or soured.

Off like a bride's nightie: To leave quickly.

Off like a bucket of prawns: To leave quickly.

Off like a robber's dog: To leave quickly.

> *"So, what made you run off like a robber's dog?" Rob asked.*
> The Family Made of Dust

Offsider: Partner or assistant.

Old chook: Derogatory term for an elderly woman (see <u>chook</u>).

Oldies: Parents.

On a good lurk: On to a good thing.

> *"We're on a good lurk."*
> The Family Made of Dust

On a good wicket: To hold a good job.

Onion grass: Also Guildford grass. A small herb with a pea-sized corm.

> *He thought he smelled blood but decided it was the onion grass.*
> The Family Made of Dust.

For more information, see *Amazing Australia.*

For recipes, see *Fairy Bread and Bush Tucker.*

On the bugle: To smell bad.

On the nod: To purchase something on credit.

On the outs: To fall into disfavor.

On the tin roof: Free of charge.

On the wallaby track: To travel from place to place looking for work (see *wallaby*).

On ya: Exclamation of encouragement.

Oodnadatta: (Aboriginal.) (Place name.) A small town in South Australia; the name means *mulga* blossom.

For more information, see *18,000 Miles.*

Opal fever: A type of obsession, similar to gold fever, that occurs when digging opal or *noodling*.

> *Although most workers usually abandoned the vein when they drew close to the border, avarice...or a bout of opal fever...could persuade them to dig far past the edges of their mine and into someone else's.*
> Woman Alone

Open slather: Golden opportunity.

Orroo: Goodbye.

OS: Overseas.

Outback: (Proper name.) The desert that covers much of Australia's interior.

> *I chucked everything to spend six months camping—alone, as a woman—in the Australian Outback.*
> Woman Alone

For more information, see *18,000 Miles.*

Outback: A remote region or secluded place.

> *Modern shopping plazas filled the flats, galleries grew alongside import stores, and an airfield whisked visitors from coastal high-rises to the outback hills.*
> The Family Made of Dust

Outstation: An Aboriginal community that isn't necessarily associated with a <u>land claim</u>.

> *"I met Angus long time ago at an outstation. No telly there, you know, no phone. No toilet to gobble up water. Just land an' quiet."*
> The Family Made of Dust

Over the fence: Unreasonable.

Oz: Australia. Derived from the Land of Oz in *The Wonderful Wizard of Oz* due to the many strange animals and plants found in the country.

For more information, see *18,000 Miles* and *Amazing Australia*.

P

Pack of poo tickets: Roll of toilet paper.
Pack your kit: To pack up all belongings.
Paddock: An enclosed pasture where livestock grazes.

> *The lame bull sharing the paddock with my tent was judged to be fat enough for slaughter.*
> Woman Alone

Pally: To be on friendly terms with (someone).
Pandanus: A genus of palm-like shrubs and trees with around 750 accepted species.

> *After breakfast, Herman led the group to a dock built across the wandering trunks of pandanus palms.*
> The Family Made of Dust

For more information, see *Amazing Australia*.

Paperbark: Also punk tree, niaouli. A type of allspice tree; name derived from the papery bark that sheds off in thick sheets.

> *He could spin a hunting boomerang so hard it would lodge in the trunk of a paperbark tree.*
> Seven Sisters

Paper yabber: Letter (see *yabber*).
Park a tiger on the rug: To vomit.
Parking bay: A small area in the *Outback* maintained by the government for travelers wishing to stop overnight.

> *My residence had actually been erected some distance from the official boundaries of the parking bay.*
> Woman Alone

For more information, see *18,000 Miles*.

Pash: To cuddle with someone or something.
Pass over the Great Divide: To die (see *Great Divide*).
Past Black Stump: In the *Outback*; in the wilderness.
Pastoralist: A sheep or cattle farmer.

> *Like some other pastoralists who were upset that sticks and stones fetched more money than beef and mutton, the man was happy to pocket a little cash to look the other way.*
> The Family Made of Dust

Pavlova, pav: Meringue dessert invented by an Australian cook as a tribute to a ballerina.

> *"And yes, you may have another slice of Pavlova."*
> The Family Made of Dust

For information and recipes, see *Fairy Bread and Bush Tucker*.

Paw-paw: Papaya.

For more information, see *Amazing Australia*.

For recipes, see *Fairy Bread and Bush Tucker*.

Peal: Excellent.

Pebble-mound mouse: A certain type of mouse that collects pebbles and builds tiny mounds around its burrow.

For more information, see *Amazing Australia*.

(to) Perve: To stare with evident lust.

Petrol: Gasoline (see also *gas, autogas*).

> *"Most of his pay went to his folks. He kept enough for petrol and food, bullets and the occasional pint."*
> The Family Made of Dust

Pickings: The bits of opal a *noodler* might find in the slag removed from a mine.

> *By the time we returned to the house, we were coated in fine white dust. Graham stored my pickings in a jar.*
> Woman Alone

Pidgin: A grammatically simplified language developed between two (or more) groups to form a shared way to communicate; ex., *Aboriginal creole* or *Kriol*.

Pie eater: A person of no importance.

Piffle: Nonsense.

Pig's bum: Wrong or incorrect.

Piker: Loner.

(to) Pinch: To arrest.

Pine: Pineapple.

For recipes, see *Fairy Bread and Bush Tucker*.

Pintupi: An Aboriginal tribe in the Western Desert cultural group.

> *The Pintupi withered so quickly even the*
> *overseer became alarmed.*
> The Family Made of Dust

Pipe clay: White clay used in traditional Aboriginal ceremonies.

> *As he sang, he mixed pipe clay with water and rubbed*
> *the paste on his two brothers.*
> Seven Sisters

Pipped at the post: To lose at the last possible second; from horse racing terminology.

Piranpa: Europeans, or any Caucasian.

> *Damn* piranpa, *he thought, always meddling.*
> The Family Made of Dust

Piss around: To fool around ineffectually, or to attempt to do something even though clearly failing.

> *He had to strap larger pieces into a harness then piss*
> *around with a real bastard of a pulley.*
> The Family Made of Dust

Pissed: Drunk.

Pissed as a parrot/toast: Very drunk.

Pissed off: Angry.

Piss in a pocket: To ingratiate yourself.

Pitchi Richi: A historical and cultural museum in *Alice Springs*.

Pitjantjatjara: An Aboriginal tribe in the Central Australian region.

> *He respected the Pitjantjatjara, to be sure, but his years at the*
> *mission had corrupted some delicate part of his spirit.*
> The Family Made of Dust

Pituri: A plant native to Australia that contains nicotine; traditionally used like tobacco for ceremonies.

> *He scrambled into a field of pituri. The wide, fleshy leaves closed*
> *over his body and trumpet-shaped flowers pattered his face*
> *as he wriggled deeper among the plants.*
> The Family Made of Dust

For more information, see *Amazing Australia*.

(the) Place of ghosts: The land of the dead in certain tribal belief systems.

> *It also said the invaders would one day*
> *return to the place of ghosts.*
> The Family Made of Dust

Play funny bunnies: To act dishonestly; to clown.

Play piano: To run fingers through a sheep's wool to find the easiest animal to shear.

Pleiades: The Pleiadian star system, a key constellation in Aboriginal *Dreamtime* tales.

> *The Pleiades, burning brightly for millennium, honor the*
> *sisterhood of mankind and the brotherhood of humanity.*
> Seven Sisters

Plonk: Cheap alcohol, usually wine (see also *lunatic soup, Nelly*).

Plum pudding, plum pud: Good, all right.

Poddy dodger: Cattle rustler.

Poets day: Friday, as in: Piss Off Early, Tomorrow's Saturday.

Pointing stick: A stick used to cast spells; used by some Aboriginal tribes (see also *point the bone, bone pointing*).

> *"He means like a pointing stick or a bone. It helps 'em*
> *cast spells, maybe put a curse on ya."*
> The Family Made of Dust

Points test: A written test given to individuals who wish to immigrate to Australia.

> *"Yes, there will be forms and yes, you will have*
> *to take the points test."*
> *"I see. And what sort of test is the points test?"*
> *"It's the points test. It rates your eligibility to*
> *enter the country in points."*
> Woman Alone

Point the bone: To wish failure upon (someone); based on the *bone pointing* curse used by certain Aboriginal tribes.

> *"No kidding, Rob. I was there. He pointed*
> *a bone. At me, remember?"*
> The Family Made of Dust

Poke mullock at: To tease (someone).

Pom, Pommy: An individual who is a citizen of England; derived from the stereotype that English people are pompous.

Pong: To stink.

Pongo: Derisive name for someone from England; based on the stereotype that the English do not bath daily (see also *dry as a Pommie's towel*).

Posh: Elegant; stylish. Can be used in a derogatory manner to describe something that seems excessively lavish or that is run down.

> *"Honestly, Dana, you always find the poshest places to land."*
> The Family Made of Dust

Possie: Position, usually a good position.

Possum guts: Coward.

(like a) Possum up a gum tree: Happy (see *gum tree*).

Postie: Mailman or woman.

Pot: A large (285 ml) glass of beer.

Potch: The milky sediment around opal that has not yet become opal.

> *Since so much time was needed for opal to mature, the immature sediment, called girasol or potch, often indicated that opal could be found.*
> Woman Alone

Prang: A car wreck.

Prezzie: Gift.

Private hotel: An establishment that takes guests but does not have a liquor license (see also *guest house, hotel, pub*).

For more information, see *18,000 Miles*.

Promite: A salty food paste used to spread on toast or sandwiches. It's basically the same thing as *Vegemite* (see) and tastes just as disgusting.

For information and recipes (if you dare), see *Fairy Bread and Bush Tucker*.

Proper: Something that is right or correct.

> *"Didn't know there were tribes in the city," the mechanic said. "Way I hear it, you [Aborigines] don't like living in proper houses."*
> The Family Made of Dust

Pub: A bar that might rent rooms (see also *guest house, hotel*).

> *All along the remote highways and even in the larger towns, pubs and roadhouses hung bulletin boards where travelers could post messages to each other.*
> Woman Alone

For more information, see *18,000 Miles*.

Pudding, pud: Dessert.

For information and recipes, see *Fairy Bread and Bush Tucker*.

Pullover: An area alongside a highway where cars can stop and campers can stay overnight for free.

ON THE WALLABY TRACK

> *At this pullover, a rocky outcropping sheltered my shiny cheeks from the neighboring trailer.*
> Woman Alone

For more information, see *18,000 Miles.*

Pull the belt in: To tighten your belt, to cut expenses.

Pull your head in: (Imperative.) Shut up; mind your own business.

Pull your socks up: (Imperative.) Get your act together.

Pure Merino: Of top quality (see *Merino*).

Pushbike: Bicycle.

Put another log on the fire: A line from a camp tune that is far too popular for any foreigner's sanity.

> *After a few beers, they whipped out a recording of their favorite camping tunes. "Put another log on the fire!" they howled.*
> Woman Alone

Put on a dingo act: To act in a cowardly manner (see *dingo*).

Put the boot in: To attack.

> *Kevin preferred a more manly approach. Put the boot in then and there, knock a few heads, and no sneaky coward tricks allowed.*
> The Family Made of Dust

Put the fangs in: To borrow money.

Put the hard word on: To proposition (someone) for sex.

Put the mockers on: To interfere with.

Put the wind up: To frighten or intimidate.

Python: Also carpet python, diamond python. A large snake that suffocates its prey by crushing it in its coils.

> *His attitude about cats meant that when a carpet python snagged one for dinner, he wasn't inclined to interfere.*
> Woman Alone

For more information, see *Amazing Australia.*

For recipes, see *Fairy Bread and Bush Tucker.*

Quandong: Also desert quandong, native peach. A hemiparasitic sandalwood plant found in the central and southern areas of Australia. The fruit of the plant is also called quandong or native peach.

> *Herman pulled the limbs from a pit-roasted wallaby then shoveled wild onions and quandongs from the bed of green leaves.*
> The Family Made of Dust

For more information, see *Amazing Australia*.

For recipes, see *Fairy Bread and Bush Tucker*.

Quartz: A clear crystal used by some tribes in ceremonial ways.

> *Their curses sent shards of wood and quartz into a victim's body, and no doctor could ease the agony.*
> The Family Made of Dust

Quid: Money.

> *"He was paid to shoot roos. He shot anything that would turn a quid."*
> The Family Made of Dust

Quids: Large sum of money.

> *"One time my mom gave me nothing but ten-cent pieces to buy my lunch all week, so everyone called me Quids."*
> The Family Made of Dust

Quirindi: (Aboriginal.) (Place name.) A small town in New South Wales; name derived from the Aboriginal word meaning "dead tree on a mountain."

For more information, see *18,000 Miles*.

R

Rabbit fence: Also rabbit-proof fence, State Barrier Fence of Western Australia, State Vermin Fence, Emu Fence. Originally built from 1901 to 1907, the three fences in Western Australia together ran 2,023 miles. They were intended to control the descendants of rabbits released by Thomas Austin in 1788.

For more information, see *18,000 Miles.*

For rabbit recipes, see *Fairy Bread and Bush Tucker.*

Race traitor: Anyone with Aboriginal ancestry who helped the government remove, kill, or harass the indigenous peoples of Australia (see also *black police*).

> *They were the worst of the race traitors, for*
> *they tracked for money alone.*
> The Family Made of Dust

Rack off: (Imperative.) Get lost.

Rafferty's rules: Chaotic; no rules at all. Possibly derived from an English dialect alteration of refractory (stubborn).

Rag: Newspaper; a loose woman.

Rainbow serpent: In certain *Dreamtime* tales, the *creator spirit* that brought all of Australia's tribes into being.

> *"The Rainbow Serpent's beard will be poison*
> *from its chin to the tip of each hair."*
> The Family Made of Dust

Rain tank: A water tank that collects rainwater; rain tanks are set at fairly regular intervals along desert highways for travelers to use.

> *I'd learned early on to refill from the rain tanks whenever possible.*
> *The water that flowed from faucets might have been safe to drink*
> *but the amount of dissolved solids made it less than palatable.*
> *Maybe Aussies drank so much tea to kill the harsh flavors.*
> Woman Alone

Ranch stay: An overnight (or longer) tourist stay at a cattle or sheep ranch.

> *Bea nodded when I mentioned the flier advertising ranch stays.*
> Woman Alone

For more information, see *18,000 Miles.*

Ratbag: Mean or eccentric person.

Raw prawn: Naive; rookie.

Razor fish: A shellfish with a long, triangular shell named for its ability to slice open waders' feet.

> *I politely declined and poked at my meal, casting about for that joker who had proclaimed razor fish edible.*
> Woman Alone

For more information, see *Amazing Australia*.

For recipes, see *Fairy Bread and Bush Tucker*.

Reckon: To believe (something); to agree (with something).

> *"Next time, you reckon we could meet in Darwin?" She lit a cigarette and winked. "You can even stay at my place."*
> The Family Made of Dust

Redback: A black spider with a red spot on its back; also the official beer of the Northern Territory, the "beer that bites you back."

> *We laughed over the fables told about the redback, a spider related to North America's black widow.*
> Woman Alone

Redback on the toilet seat: A line from a popular tune that marks the amusing yet real danger of being bitten on the butt while using the toilet.

Red, black and gold: The colors of the *Aboriginal flag*; also used as a term to denote the Aboriginal flag itself.

Rellie: Relative.

Ridgy-didge, ridgie-didgie: The genuine article; honest.

Right: All right; to be OK. Also used to denote that something is of good or useful quality.

> *"It's the bladder from a wine box. You know, those liters you throw in the fridge? After you empty it out, a puff or two of air turns it into a right nice pillow for when you're in the water!"*
> Woman Alone

Righto: Expression of agreement.

Ringer: Experienced sheep shearer.

Ripe: Spoiled; overripe.

Ripper: Fantastic.

River peppermint: Also river white gum. A type of tree with rough bark that sheds higher up the trunk, the leaves of which are distilled for piperitone essential oil.

For more information, see *Amazing Australia*.

Roadhouse: A single building alongside remote roads that offers one or more of the following services: *petrol*, shower facilities, bathrooms, a snack or grocery selection, room rental.

> *The first night, I stopped at a roadhouse intending to pitch my tent nearby. The rough-looking men who hung around in the parking lot drinking had little to do except watch me.*
> Woman Alone

For more information, see *18,000 Miles*.

Road train: Semi truck hauling up to three trailers. Due to their length, they can be difficult to pass on the outback roads.

> *A road train loomed ahead. The roadbed was raised, and I saw a line of vehicles sitting behind the tractor trailer.*
> Woman Alone

For more information, see *18,000 Miles*.

Roaring: Brisk; fantastic.

Rock hole: A depression in a rock that is of note due to its tendency to collect water.

> *The rock holes near his house were black and as still as a sheet hung to dry.*
> The Family Made of Dust

Rock pool: A pool of water that has collected in a depression in a rock; due to the importance of water for traditional peoples, rock pools that were visited regularly might hold anything from a few sips to thousands of gallons.

> *There was the sulfuric tinge of boulders shedding their rinds, the purple of sandstone like engorged beef, dead-white saltpans and the sepia fringe around a rock pool.*
> The Family Made of Dust

Rollie: A hand-rolled cigarette.

Rolling: Drunk.

Roo: Kangaroo (see also *boomer*, *flier*).

> *"Dennis tracked roos hoping to lay a trap along a game trail but neither of us has actually seen any animals since we broke down."*
> Woman Alone

For more information, see *Amazing Australia*.

For recipes, see *Fairy Bread and Bush Tucker*.

Roo bar: Steel bars bolted in front of a car's bumper to protect the grill from collisions with kangaroos, *brumbies* (see *brumby*), or cattle.

> *Hit 'em so hard, the roo bar breaks. Hit
> 'em so hard, the fender shakes.*
> The Family Made of Dust

Roo shooter: Government-paid kangaroo culler (see also *dog stiffener*).

> *To a rancher beleaguered by drought and debt, every blade
> eaten by native animals robbed them of beef.
> Roo shooters were always welcome.*
> The Family Made of Dust

Root: To engage in sex.

Rooted: Exhausted.

Ropable: Angry.

Rotten: Drunk.

Rough as bags: Unrefined.

Rough end of the pineapple: A bad deal; the short end of the stick.

Royal Flying Doctor: A flying ambulance that is often the only way to access emergency medical assistance in the *Outback*.

> *The Royal Flying Doctor ... arrived within
> an unexpectedly short two hours.*
> Woman Alone

RS: Abbreviation for *rat shit*, meaning bad.

Rug up: To dress warmly.

Run the rabbit: A beer or liquor run made after selling hours have closed.

S

Salad: A few leaves of lettuce that top a sandwich; can be confusing for tourists expecting a salad alongside their sandwich.

> "Tell me, what's your favorite dinner?"
> "Oh, an egg sandwich with lots of salad."
> The Family Made of Dust

For recipes, see *Fairy Bread and Bush Tucker*.

Saltbush: A common blue-gray shrub, the seeds of which were used as food by Aboriginal tribes.

> *Khaki saltbush reminded him of parasitic fish that drained the color from the land for their own dull leaves.*
> The Family Made of Dust

For more information, see *Amazing Australia*.

For recipes, see *Fairy Bread and Bush Tucker*.

Saltie: A saltwater crocodile (see also *freshie*, *croc*).

For more information, see *Amazing Australia*.

For recipes, see *Fairy Bread and Bush Tucker*.

Sammie: Sandwich.

For recipes, see *Fairy Bread and Bush Tucker*.

Sand fly: Also sandfly, sand flea. Any genus of biting or blood-sucking fly encountered in sandy areas.

For more information, see *Amazing Australia*.

Sandgroper: Resident of Western Australia; derived from the native burrowing insect found there.

Sand shoes: Sneakers.

(one) Sandwich short of a picnic: Stupid.

Sanger: Sandwich.

For recipes, see *Fairy Bread and Bush Tucker*.

Sauce: Ketchup (see also *dead horse*).

For recipes, see *Fairy Bread and Bush Tucker*.

Scallops: Fried potato cakes.

For recipes, see *Fairy Bread and Bush Tucker*.

School: Group of drinkers.

Scone: A person's head.

Screw palm: See *pandanus*.

Scroggin: Trail mix.

For recipes, see *Fairy Bread and Bush Tucker.*

Scrub: Any native bushes or shrubs that grow wild; also any remote area or region.

> The flat plains wore the extravagance of distance and simplicity. What little scrub did manage to grow crouched low beneath the sun.
> Woman Alone

Scrubber: Dirty or low person.

Scrub itch: Parasitic skin mites contracted by bathing in tropical waters; an infestation is characterized by a ring of itchy, red welts, usually on the abdomen.

For more information, see *Amazing Australia.*

Scrub tick: Any of 75 species of ticks native to Australia, one of which can cause paralysis.

For more information, see *Amazing Australia.*

Scrub turkey: Also brushturkey, brush-turkey, Australian brushturkey, bush turkey. A common Megapodiidae, black with a red head and yellow neck ring, found in eastern Australia.

> Not long after we had settled in, a scrub turkey had come out of the woods to investigate.
> Woman Alone

For more information, see *Amazing Australia.*

Sealed: Paved. Might indicate that a dirt road has been sprayed with oil to keep the dust down.

For more information, see *18,000 Miles.*

Sea snake: Also coral reef snake. One of several members of a subfamily that are venomous and mostly unable to move on land.

> We spotted a sea snake, a wiggly, intuitive line that drew and erased itself on the watery blackboard.
> Woman Alone

For more information, see *Amazing Australia.*

Seedcake: A patty made from the ground seeds of various wild seeds.

> She offered him wild oranges and seedcakes but he ate only meat.
> Seven Sisters

For recipes, see *Fairy Bread and Bush Tucker.*

Seen its last gumtree: Dead (see *gumtree*).

See you in the soup: See you around.

Senior man: An Aboriginal man who has been recognized by his tribe to have obtained a high level of *Dreaming* knowledge.

> *The senior men and women knew the girls as wards to be cared for, as young minds that were curious yet lacking in experience.*
> Seven Sisters

Senior woman: An Aboriginal woman who has been recognized by her tribe to have obtained a high level of *Dreaming* knowledge.

> *Senior women considered the emotional and psychological needs of individuals and the group.*
> Seven Sisters

Seppo: A derogatory nickname for an American; perhaps from use of "septic tank," itself from rhyming slang (*Yank*).

Serviette: Napkin.

Settler's clock: *Kookaburra*; (see also *breakfast bird*).
  For more information, see *Amazing Australia*.

Seven Sisters: The Pleiades; also the seven *Dreamtime* sisters who proved their strength by undergoing *man-making* ceremonies.

> *The seven sisters are extraordinary because they balanced different kinds of knowledge within themselves.*
> Seven Sisters

Shag: A *cormorant*; also intercourse.
  For more information on the bird, see *Amazing Australia*.

(like a) Shag on a rock: Forlorn; lonely (see *shag*).

Shark biscuit: A novice surfer; a swimmer who goes out too far.

Shaver: A child.

Shearer's joy: Beer.

Sheila: A woman.

> *"I didn't know a sheila could drive like that!"*
> Woman Alone

Shepherd's friend: A *dingo*. Ironic term derived from the belief that dingoes hang around flocks hoping to eat sheep and lambs.

Shickered: Drunk.

Shiny ass: Government worker; derived from the stereotype that government employees are lazy and spend all their time sitting around.

Shiralee: Sleeping bag (see also *swag*).

Shirty: To be upset or angry.

Shivoo: Loud party.
Shonky: Very suspicious.
Shook on: Stuck on, as in love or infatuation.
Shoot through: To pass through in a hurry.
Shop: A store.

> *Almost every foray to the shops was an opportunity to discover another stray.*
> Woman Alone

Short of numbers in the Upper House: Stupid, from Parliamentary proceedings that require a certain number of votes to pass a motion.
Shortwave: Radio network that operates in a limited area; used to broadcast school lessons to students who live too far away from school to attend class.
Shot full of holes: Drunk.
Shout: To buy something for someone, usually a drink.

> *What friendly employer wouldn't shout his pals a round?*
> Woman Alone

Shove off: (Imperative.) Go away.
Sickie: Sick day taken for reasons other than health, usually to pursue a hobby or relax.
Silly as a wet hen/a wheel: Crazy; vacuous.
Silly season: Christmas.
Since cockie was an egg: A long time (see *cockie*).
(to) Sing: To call on the power of the *Dreamtime* energy; also to cast a spell or curse on someone.

> *A man sang a song they had never heard before then told the girls to sing.*
> Seven Sisters

Sink the boot: To attack viciously (see *put the boot in*).
Sit up like Jackie: To stand out in a crowd.
Skin: Tribal affiliation.

> *"What's your skin? What tribe are you from?"*
> The Family Made of Dust

Skin name: A special name given to an individual that connects them to a specific element of *Dreamtime* energy.

> *"If you know someone's skin name, you know
> how you're related to that person."*
> The Family Made of Dust

Skip, Skippy: Derogatory term for an Australian, from a popular television series in which a kangaroo named Skippy performed heroic deeds (similar to Lassie).

Skite: To boast or brag.

Sky spirit: The *Dreamtime* spirits that live in the sky.

> *As the oldest sister joined the ensuing celebration, she
> felt the eyes of the sky spirits on her.*
> Seven Sisters

Sky world: The celestial place where the *sky spirits* live.

> *"This was a spirit tree, where the dead climb up to the sky world."*
> The Family Made of Dust

Slag: To break apart.

Slash: To urinate (usually said of a male).

Slow as a wet weekend: Painfully slow.

Smack a blue: To run into trouble.

(to) Smoke: To smudge a person or thing; that is, to purify a person or thing with the smoke of smoldering materials.

> *"Our healer will be by later. He'll smoke you
> then we'll all have dinner."*
> The Family Made of Dust

Smoko: Morning coffee break.

> *We stopped at his house for smoko, a sort of coffee break
> with a mini-meal. His wife Tess fed us flapjacks
> smeared with syrup and butter.*
> Woman Alone

For recipes, see *Fairy Bread and Bush Tucker*.

Snag: Sausage.

For recipes, see *Fairy Bread and Bush Tucker*.

Snag short of a barbie: Slow-witted (see *snag*, *barbie*).

Snake-necked turtle: Also side-neck turtle. One of three living families of turtle that folds its neck sideways into its shell.

> *Gabe was famished, yet he ate carefully. He learned the name of the snake-necked turtle and how it was prized for its fat.*
> The Family Made of Dust

For more information, see *Amazing Australia*.

For mock turtle recipes, see *Fairy Bread and Bush Tucker*.

Snakey: To be upset.

Snappy gum: Also scribbly gum. A tree native to eastern Australia with scribbled lines appearing on its bark.

> *Not far from the ridge stood a cluster of snappy gums.*
> The Family Made of Dust

For more information, see *Amazing Australia*.

Snout on: To have a grudge toward (someone).

Soap tree: Also red ash. A species of Rhamnaceae with leaves that can be rubbed in water to produce a soapy liquid that cleans hands.

> *By the time we arrived, the three Aboriginal women had stripped leaves from a soap tree.*
> Woman Alone

For more information, see *Amazing Australia*.

Solanum: A small fruit (see *bush tomato*) that tastes like melon; also the plant on which the fruit grows.

> *He broke the skewers and trampled the dried Solanums.*
> Seven Sisters

For more information, see *Amazing Australia*.

For recipes, see *Fairy Bread and Bush Tucker*.

Song: A *Dreamtime* tale set to music; songs and the act of *singing* can call up the Dreamtime energy.

> *Generations offered their dead, carved new symbols and sang the eternal songs.*
> The Family Made of Dust

Song keeper: A man or woman who is responsible for safeguarding a specific element of *Dreamtime* energy on behalf of the tribe.

> *Only other song keepers who died without passing*
> *on their skills would understand.*
> The Family Made of Dust

Songlines: The stories that describe the creation of specific places, animals or plants and the *Dreamtime* energy held within each.

> *After walking those songlines myself, I returned to the United*
> *States with a very different perspective.*
> Seven Sisters

Songman, songwoman: A man or woman who is the keeper of one or more *Dreamtime* stories.

> *The songwoman gasped. A dingo stood at the back door.*
> The Family Made of Dust

Sook: Crybaby.

Sooky: Sniveling, whiney.

Sorry cut: A self-inflicted wound cut into the scalp or skin to express grief or sorrow; also used as a way to offer a deeply heartfelt apology in traditional Aboriginal culture.

> *A sorry cut, a little wound to let out blood,*
> *evened out the suffering.*
> The Family Made of Dust

Sort it: To fix (something).

Southern buster: Cool southern wind blowing into Sydney during the summer.

Southern Cross: (Proper name.) The constellation Crux, located in a bright portion of the Milky Way.

Spark: Electrician.

Speed merchant: Reckless or fast driver.

Speewa: Any remote area.

Spieler: Con artist.

Spinifex: A hummock-forming grass of the genus *Triodia* that bristles with silica shards and cuts skin like pulverized grass.

> *His arms and legs were spindly things that stuck out every*
> *which way like spinifex grass.*
> Seven Sisters

For more information, see *Amazing Australia*.

Spinifex mouse: Also spinifex hopping mouse, tarkawara, tarrkawarra. A primarily nocturnal mouse with elongated hind legs and a brush-tipped tail.

> *His mother's complexion, so pale as to make any other man sallow, had mixed with Bret's iron-gray cast. The result lay somewhere between honey and cream, like the fur of a spinifex mouse.*
> The Family Made of Dust

For more information, see *Amazing Australia*.

Spinifex resin: The gum coating found on certain species of Spinifex grasses; traditionally used to make Aboriginal tools and as a binder for paint.

For more information, see *Amazing Australia*.

Spiny echidna: Also spiny anteater, *echidna*.

> *They mustered every wallaby and kangaroo, every crocodile and goanna, every rat and mouse and spiny echidna and snake.*
> Seven Sisters

For more information, see *Amazing Australia*.

Spirit board: An oblong board pointed at both ends that has been carved or painted with *Dreaming* symbols.

> *Before attacking the men, the sorcerer had painted the spirit board and dressed it in hairstring.*
> The Family Made of Dust

Spirit of death: A bat; derived from a *Dreamtime* story about a man who murdered his wives and was punished by being turned into a bat.

> *The lies he shrieked about his wives pitched so high people could no longer hear them. To this day, the bat is still called the spirit of death.*
> Seven Sisters

For more information, see *Amazing Australia*.

Spirit tree: A tree that connects the earth to the *sky world*, up which human souls travel after death.

> *[To steal] the spirit tree, Dana had also enlisted the help of the rancher who ran the property.*
> The Family Made of Dust

Spitfire: The baghouse moth caterpillar, named for the burning wounds it can cause to human skin.

> *Also known as the spitfire, the baghouse moth caterpillar fed on acacia trees.*
> Woman Alone

For more information, see *Amazing Australia*.

Spit the dummie: To become upset; from a baby's tendency to cry when it loses its dummy, or pacifier.

Spitting chips: Angry (as in: spitting nails).

Sprog: Child.

Sprung: To be caught doing something you ought not to do.

Spunk: Good-looking person.

Spunky: Attractive, good looking.

Spur: A dirt track that feeds off of a main or paved road; often used as shortcuts.

> *The long dirt roads known as spurs, most of which could only be accessed using a four-wheel-drive vehicle, were marked, which made the map detailed enough.*
> Woman Alone

Square off: To apologize or make up.

Squib: Small firecracker.

Stable fly: A biting, blood-feeding fly that has become a pest in Western Australia, particularly along the coastal areas.

For more information, see *Amazing Australia*.

Starkers: Naked (i.e., stark naked).

For information on nude beaches, see *18,000 Miles*.

Starve the lizards: Exclamation of disbelief or awe.

Station: A ranch.

> *The cattle station consisted of thousands of acres leased from the government, a common arrangement in a land too poor to support cattle efficiently.*
> Woman Alone

Sticky beak: Nosy person.

Stick your bib in: To be nosy.

Stinger: A jellyfish.

For more information, see *Amazing Australia*.

Stinging gimpy: A type of bush with caustic sap that can cause burn wounds.

> *"I see you're taking your kids," he said. "Keep a close eye on them. They can disappear in a flash in that thick brush. And don't let them touch nothing, either. You know about the stinging gimpy bush?"*
> Woman Alone

For more information, see *Amazing Australia*.

Stinging nasties: Collective term for any biting or virulent pest such as insects, spiders, or snakes (see also *bities*).

For more information, see *Amazing Australia*.

Stir the possum: To stir up trouble.

Stockmen: Wandering individuals who appear to be up to no good; originally hired ranch hands who needed to move from one ranch to another when their jobs were over.

Stolen Generations: Also Stolen Children. The children of Australian Aboriginal and Torres Strait Islander parents who were forcibly removed from their families in an attempt to eliminate their race.

Her whisper-fine hair had been his obsession until she wrapped it in black bandanas to honor the Stolen Generation, dead to their culture.
The Family Made of Dust

Stonefish: A genus of fish with sharp spines that contain a highly venomous toxin fatal to humans.

We were told to move forward no further than where he stood to avoid the deadly spines of stonefish.
Woman Alone

For more information, see *Amazing Australia*.

Stone the crows: Expression of amazement.

Stoney: Flat broke.

Storm stick: Umbrella.

Stoush: Fight; to hit.

Streak: Tall or lean person.

Strewth: Exclamation of surprise or shock.

Strides: Pants.

Strike a light: Exclamation of disbelief.

Strine: The Australian slang word for Australian slang.

String belt: A belt made from human hair and plant fiber or animal fur used for Aboriginal ceremonies.

He wore only a string belt, a pair of shorts, and bands on his arms and legs.
The Family Made of Dust

Stringybark: One of many Eucalyptus tree species with a thick, fibrous bark; because the term is descriptive, not all stringybark trees are closely related.

> *There came a day when his rifle lay untouched. That morning his father parked beneath a stand of stringybark on the crest of a hill.*
> The Family Made of Dust

For more information, see *Amazing Australia*.

Stroppy: To be in a bad mood.

Sturt's Desert Pea: An arid wildflower well known for its unusual flowers.

> *The small garden planted in front of the main building included the spectacular Stuart's Desert Pea. ... An Aboriginal story said the petals were the blood of a family that had been murdered as they slept.*
> Woman Alone

For more information, see *Amazing Australia*.

Stubbie, stubby: A bottle of beer; an especially short pair of men's shorts.

Stuff about: Also stuff around. To mess around.

> *"He could have killed me any time. Why stuff around like this?"*
> The Family Made of Dust

Stuff all: Nothing.

Stuffed: Broken.

Stuff up: To make a mistake.

(like a) Stunned mullet: To be confused; to act dazed or to be preoccupied and therefore not engaged in what's happening.

> *"Oh, don't act like a stunned mullet!" she laughed.*
> The Family Made of Dust

Suck: A suck-up.

Sugarbag: The honey created by Australia's stingless native bees.

> *If Ben found a nest, he would return to the house for a container and harvest the sugarbag.*
> Woman Alone

For recipes, see *Fairy Bread and Bush Tucker*.

Sulphur-crested cockatoo: A large white *cockatoo* that inhabits wooded areas of Australia and New Guinea.

> *Sulphur-crested cockatoos were much larger and much noisier. Whenever I disturbed them, the flocks exploded into the sky to scream their protests.*
> Woman Alone

For more information, see *Amazing Australia*.

Sunbake: To sunbathe.

Sunday dog: Lazy person.

Surfies: Surfers.

Sus, suss: To be untrustworthy; also to examine something in order to determine the truth.

Swag: A bag or tarp that protects a sleeping bag or bedroll; also the sleeping bag or bedroll.

> *Other travelers gave us a quick nod as they continued stuffing their 4WD truck with an assortment of packs and swags.*
> Woman Alone

Swagman: Hobo, wanderer.

Sweet cop: Easy task or job.

Swimmers: Swimsuit.

> *"You sure do fill out those swimmers right nice," he called.*
> Woman Alone

T

Ta: Thanks.

Tablelands: Also Atherton Tableland. A plateau in the Great Dividing Range in tropical Queensland.

> *"Oh, I'm really enjoying this," I said.*
> *"Especially after a few weeks in the rain."*
> *"Up in the tablelands, were you?"*
> Woman Alone

For more information, see *18,000 Miles*.

Take a punt: Take a chance.

Take-away: Fast food or takeout food.

Take the mickey out of: To tease (someone).

Talk a glass eye to sleep: Boring.

Talk the leg off an iron pot: To talk a lot.

> *"Selena talked the leg off an iron pot once." Rob winked and flopped down on the grass.*
> The Family Made of Dust

Tall poppy: Self-important person; i.e., the one poppy that grows taller than the rest.

Tall white: Also flat white. A beverage made with espresso and steamed milk; similar to a cappuccino or latte but smaller in volume and with a higher coffee-to-milk ratio.

For information and recipes, see *Fairy Bread and Bush Tucker*.

Tasmanian tiger: A marsupial much like a dog in appearance that is extinct but which, various sightings claim, has been spotted during recent decades.

> *One drawing depicted the thylacine, the Tasmanian tiger, complete with stripes across the flanks.*
> Woman Alone

For more information, see *Amazing Australia*.

Tea: Dinner; the evening meal.

For recipes, see *Fairy Bread and Bush Tucker*.

Tee-up: To make an appointment; to organize or arrange.

Ten-ounce sandwich: A beer drunk in place of a proper meal (see also <u>*emu's breakfast, duck's dinner*</u>).

Test: Rugby match.

That's the way the Violet Crumbles: Expression meaning "that's life" (see *Violet Crumble*).

Thingo: Thingamajig.

Things are crook in Musclebrook/at Tallarook: Things are bad; something's fishy.

Thongs: Flip-flops.

> *The pair fled, their thongs clapping like wings.*
> The Family Made of Dust

Three-dollar bill: Said of something that is strange.

Three pots short of a shout: Stupid (see *pot, shout*).

Through the middle: The journey through the middle of the continent, usually performed on a north-south axis.

> *The Danes and I burst out laughing.*
> *"Four cylinders," yapped one as his blond curls flapped.*
> *"That is no good. Not up the middle."*
> *"You want big car," agreed the darkest Dane....*
> Woman Alone

Thugby: Derisive name for rugby.

Thump: A punch.

> *"And even if I tried something then all you'd have to do is thump my chest and down I'd go. Not much longer for it, not me."*
> Woman Alone

Thylacine: The *Tasmanian tiger*.

For more information, see *Amazing Australia*.

Tickle the till: To steal.

Tight as a fish's ass: Stingy.

Tin, tinned: Canned, as in canned food.

> *Yancy offered five dollars and a case of tinned meat as payment.*
> The Family Made of Dust

Tin assed: Lucky, often said derisively when someone is jealous of another person's luck.

Tin eared: Eavesdropper.

Tingle: Telephone call.

Tinnie: Can of beer.

Tizz: Excessive excitement.

Tjukurpa: (Aboriginal.) For the *Anangu* tribe, the creation period of the *Dreamtime*.

> *In the* Tjukurpa, *the ancestors created things by calling out their names. In that single act the flower bloomed, the lizard ran, water flowed.*
> The Family Made of Dust

Tjulpun-tjulpunpa: (Aboriginal.) The *Pitjantjatjara* word for flowers or wildflowers.

> *Depending on the country and the season, he might gather plant silk from the fist-sized nuts of the kapok tree or from* tjulpun-tjulpunpa, *wildflowers like daisy and billy button.*
> The Family Made of Dust

For more information, see *Amazing Australia*.

(to have) Tickets on him/herself: Indicates that someone thinks highly of him/herself.

Too right: Totally.

Top End: The Northern Territory.

For more information, see *18,000 Miles*.

Torch: Flashlight.

Totem: A natural item, animal, plant, or even a weather event assigned to an individual at birth and that functions as their spiritual symbol.

> *The woman who had dreamed his spirit totem, whose color he wore on his hands and face and chest and thighs. If he had stayed with her, he might have learned of Dreaming and of songs.*
> The Family Made of Dust

Tracker: An expert at following the trails and signs left by animals or people.

> *Trackers worked rock and river where no European could find life, let alone the signs it left behind.*
> The Family Made of Dust

Tree of Life: A *spirit tree*.

> *Bev said the station owner who had given them the Tree of Life was calling every hour.*
> The Family Made of Dust

Trimmer: Excellent.

Truckie: A truck driver.

> *"Dennis hitched a ride with a truckie to call the road service but the closest garage is in Mt. Isa."*
> Woman Alone

True blue: Genuine, the real thing.

Truffle: A species native to Australia that isn't as flavorful as the better-known truffles found in other countries.

> *The apricot-sized pitted stones that were said to be the fossilized truffles had been carted away.*
> The Family Made of Dust

For more information, see *Amazing Australia.*

For recipes, see *Fairy Bread and Bush Tucker.*

Tube: Large can of beer.

Tucker: Food (see *bush tucker*).

> *"I run tourists into the desert to find tucker. No hunting, mind. We pick fruit, dig roots, and find the occasional grub."*
> The Family Made of Dust

For recipes, see *Fairy Bread and Bush Tucker.*

Tucker chute: Mouth (see *tucker*).

Tuckshop: Cafeteria or eatery (see *tucker*).

Tumble to: To catch on to (something).

Turn dingo: To become an informant (see *dingo*).

Turn it up: (Imperative.) Stop; pay attention; wake up to what's really going on.

Turps: Turpentine; alcohol.

Twins: Two offspring produced by the same pregnancy. Traditionally considered the result of a curse because having twins increased the danger to the mother.

> *His desire was too palpable, his lust too ravenous. Surely even peeking through a crack at him would curse a woman with twins.*
> Seven Sisters

Two-bob lair: Cheap, tacky (see *lair*).

(like a) Two-bob watch: Quickly or erratically (i.e., like a cheap watch).

Two-pot screamer: Someone who gets drunk easily (see *pot*).

Two-up: Gambling game played with two coins; bets are placed on the outcome of one flip of both coins. Illegal except at the Australian Two-Up School and casinos.

Two-way radio: The CB (citizens band) radio.

The gawping commenced, I glowered again, and a few seconds were snatched to [continue my shower]. Then a third bus arrived, forcing me to wait again. Ah, the wonders of two-way radio.
Woman Alone

U

Uluru: Also *Ayer's Rock*. A large sandstone formation in the heart of Australia.

> *Tiddalick was already as big as Uluru, that giant stone in the middle of the desert. No one could force him to do anything.*
> Seven Sisters

For more information, see *18,000 Miles*.

Underdaks: Underwear (see *daks*).

Underground mutton: Rabbit.

For more information, see *Amazing Australia*.

For recipes, see *Fairy Bread and Bush Tucker*.

Under the lap: Off the books, unofficial.

Uni: College or university.

Up a gumtree: In trouble (see *gumtree*).

Up the duff: Pregnant.

Up the pole: Confused; incorrect.

Up the spout: Pregnant; ruined.

Up yourself: To be full of yourself.

Urunga: (Aboriginal.) (Place name.) A small town in New South Wales; the name means "long beach."

For more information, see *18,000 Miles*.

Ute: Utility truck.

V

VB: Victoria Bitter, a brand of beer.

> *"V.B. V!B!" he yelled quite clearly.* "V.B. beer, Victoria Bitter!"
> Woman Alone

For more information, see *Fairy Bread and Bush Tucker.*

Vegemite: Yeast spread extracted from vegetables. Tastes salty and is unbelievably gross (see also *Marmite*, *Promite*).

> "Maybe they like Vegemite."
> "No accounting for taste."
> The Family Made of Dust

For more information and recipes (if you dare), see *Fairy Bread and Bush Tucker.*

Veggie: Vegetarian.

Violet Crumble: Candy bar similar to malted milk balls.

For more information, see *Fairy Bread and Bush Tucker.*

W

Wacker: Crazy or eccentric person.

Waddy: A club made of dense, heavy wood used as a weapon (see *nulla nulla*).

Waffle: Nonsense.

Wag: To skip school.

Waidup: (Aboriginal.) Water during the *dry* season.

Walkabout: To wander through the wilderness.

> "He's finally gone walkabout." Bret's teeth formed a glittery, slippery sort of smile. "That's no surprise. He always struck me as wild."
> The Family Made of Dust

Walkover: Easy.

Wallaby: A small- to medium-sized macropod native to Australia and New Guinea.

> Whenever a hunter gave her a cut of kangaroo or wallaby, she took that up to the plateau.
> Seven Sisters

For more information, see *Amazing Australia*.

Walla-Walla: Remote area.

Walloper: Police officer; from the idea that police wallop, or strike, people.

Wally: Klutz; someone who repeats the same mistakes.

Waltzing matilda: To carry a swag or bedroll (see *matilda*).

Wanampi: (Aboriginal.) The *Rainbow Serpent* that sleeps under *Uluru*.

> When Wanampi woke, Dana would be ready.
> The Family Made of Dust

Wanker: Jerk.

> "If I've enough money for a bucket of prawns, I'd be a silly wanker to ruin 'em on the barbie!"
> Woman Alone

Waratah: Also Queensland tree waratah, red silky oak waratah tree. A tropical rainforest tree that produces large clusters of orange-red flowers; also a genus of shrubs with five species native to Australia that produces large, showy flowers.

> *He always napped under a certain waratah*
> *tree far from any camp noise.*
> Seven Sisters

For more information, see *Amazing Australia*.

Warumungu: (Aboriginal.) An Aboriginal people who live around Tennant Creek and *Alice Springs* in the Northern Territory.

> *Some two hundred Warumungu were corralled*
> *at the Phillip Creek settlement.*
> The Family Made of Dust

Water biscuit: Saltine.

Water buffalo: The Asian water buffalo, introduced between 1824 and 1849, is feral in the Northern Territory.

> *Although the temperament of domesticated breeds was somewhat*
> *less touchy than the wild water buffalo in Australia's northern*
> *regions, any animal that size deserved respect.*
> Woman Alone

For more information, see *Amazing Australia*.

For recipes, see *Fairy Bread and Bush Tucker*.

Wattle: Also golden wattle. An *acacia* tree native to southeastern Australia.

> *He thought of the wattle blossoms that lit the desert every spring,*
> *of how the brightest parts of nature were always the shortest lived.*
> The Family Made of Dust

For more information, see *Amazing Australia*.

Weatherboard: Wooden house.

Weaver ant: Also *green ants*.

> *Papery wildflowers grew between the plants and the air*
> *had the sweet bite of a weaver ant nest.*
> The Family Made of Dust

For more information, see *Amazing Australia*.

For recipes, see *Fairy Bread and Bush Tucker*.

Wedding tackle: A man's genitals.

(the) Welfare: Social services.

> *"The welfare took me when I was three,"* he said. *"I was held at the Central Brethren's Mission before they shipped me north."*
> The Family Made of Dust

Well under: Drunk.

Wet: The rainy season. (Also see *dry*.)

> *Low-lying areas that flooded during the wet season were also off limits.*
> Seven Sisters

For more information, see *18,000 Miles*.

Wharfie: Dock worker.

What is this, bush week: Sarcastic question asked when someone has done something stupid.

What's crawling on you: Question asked of unreasonable or cranky person.

> *"What the hell is crawling on you?"*
> The Family Made of Dust

Where crows fly backward: The *Outback*, where it is said that crows fly backward to keep the dust out of their eyes.

Whinge: To complain.

Whinger: A chronic complainer.

Whinging Pom: Derogatory term based on the stereotype that English people complain chronically (see *Pom*).

Whip around: To collect money to benefit another.

White ant: A termite.

For more information, see *Amazing Australia*.

For recipes, see *Fairy Bread and Bush Tucker*.

White ants: Crazy; derived from the behavior of the *white ant*.

> *"We were waving our hats and shouting like we were as crazy as white ants!"*
> Woman Alone

White pointer: Highway patrol.

Wild orange: Also native orange. A tree related to capers; also the fruit produced by the tree.

> *"What's your best meal?"* ...
> *"Roast bustard with wild orange sauce."*
> The Family Made of Dust

For more information, see *Amazing Australia*.

For recipes, see *Fairy Bread and Bush Tucker*.

Willy-nilly: Dust devil; untidy.

Willy wagtail: Also willie wagtail. A piebald passerine native to Australia, New Guinea, and nearby islands.

---
*Willy Wagtail and Cockatoo stepped in with
their own type of clowning.*
Seven Sisters

For more information, see *Amazing Australia*.

Wind spirit: The *Dreamtime* spirits that live inside the wind.

---
*The wind spirits happened to brush against the bachelor just then.
They immediately knew his intention.*
Seven Sisters

Wirrie: (Aboriginal.) Also wirri. A weapon that can be used as a club or a missile. From the Gaurna language.

Dana spread out the tools of his magic, and beside those, tools for killing. First was the flint knife he had shaped as Tjamu had taught him so long ago. Then he set out the rifle, the same .22 that had brought the roo shooter to his knees. Finally came the wirrie.
The Family Made of Dust

Witchetty bush: Also wanderrie *wattle*, granite wattle. A Mimosiodeae shrub that often hosts the *witchetty grub*.

---
*Witchetty grubs were found, not surprisingly,
wherever the witchetty bush grew.*
Woman Alone

For more information, see *Amazing Australia*.

Witchetty grub: Also witchety, witjuti. The gigantic wood-eating larvae of several types of moths that were an important source of protein.

Whatever the mother had gathered—witchetty grubs, succulent lizards and bustard eggs—disappeared into her son's mouth.
Seven Sisters

For more information, see *Amazing Australia*.

For recipes, see *Fairy Bread and Bush Tucker*.

Within coo-ee: Close by, within calling distance (see *coo-ee*).

Wobbly: Temper tantrum; to "chuck a wobbly."

Woffle dust: Luck. When hoping for a good dice roll or card deal, you "put a bit of woffle dust" on the cards or the die.

Wog: The flu; derisive term for foreigner.

Wollybutt: A type of eucalyptus tree.

> *Then came open woodlands dominated by wollybutts, eucalypts with flowers of fire. The stamens smelled so sweet Zack crushed the sticky clusters against the roof of his mouth.*
> The Family Made of Dust

For more information, see *Amazing Australia*.

Woman-making: Traditional Aboriginal ceremonies associated with a girl's coming-of-age.

> *She wondered if other boys or even men thought the woman-making rite was less valuable.*
> Seven Sisters

Wombat: One of three marsupial species that dig burrows with their powerful claws.

> *In the evening, after the dingoes and wombats and bats had paid their respects, came silence.*
> Woman Alone

For more information, see *Amazing Australia*.

Women's business: The spiritual and ceremonial issues associated with a woman's way of life.

> *"And you shouldn't be looking over there, Gabe. That's women's business, strictly off limits to us blokes."*
> The Family Made of Dust

Woomera: Aboriginal spear thrower. Woomeras effectively extended the length of a person's arm, greatly improving the force with which a spear could be thrown.

> *He talked of stealing the women's tools, of men carving their own woomeras and hardening their own spears.*
> Seven Sisters

Woop Woop: The *Outback*; also any remote region or isolated place (see *outback*).

Woop-Woop pigeon: *Kookaburra* (see also *breakfast bird*).

For more information, see *Amazing Australia*.

Wouldn't be dead for quids: Feeling great (see *quids*).

Wouldn't have a bar of: Wouldn't be involved in (something).

Wouldn't in a pink fit: Wouldn't be involved in (something).

Wouldn't shout in a shark attack: Tight-fisted (see *shout*).

Wowser: Repressed person.

Wrong-way: A relationship or activity that breaks taboos in Aboriginal society.

> *Any wrong-way act disrupted the flow of energy and threatened the clans, their land, and the survival of the entire world.*
> Seven Sisters

Xantippe: (Aboriginal.) (Place name.) A small town in Western Australia; the name translates as "looking for water from a deeper well." The rock holes, known as Gnamma holes, were featured in the movie *The Rabbit Proof Fence.*

X-ray: A style of painting in traditional Aboriginal art that began in <u>Arnhem Land</u> around 2000 BC. The style depicts the internal organs and bones of animals and people.

XXXX: Pronounced "Four X" or "barbed wire." The official beer of Queensland.

Y

Yabber: To talk.

Yabby: Also yabbie. A freshwater crayfish, very large, that is often kept as a pet; also the ghost shrimp.

> *The yabby was sweet and earthy, unlike the briny crab of the coast.*
> The Family Made of Dust

For more information, see *Amazing Australia*.

For recipes, see *Fairy Bread and Bush Tucker*.

Yagga: (Aboriginal.) Quiet.

Yakka: Work.

Yalke: (Aboriginal.) *Onion grass*.

> *Back at camp, Rob pulled a box of dried fruit from the trunk. He reconstituted screws of garlic, apple rings and a resinous clump of bean paste to rub on the meat then buried the* yalke *in the embers.*
> The Family Made of Dust

For more information, see *Amazing Australia*.

For recipes, see *Fairy Bread and Bush Tucker*.

Yandy: To winnow seeds from chaff or dust.

> *She yandied enough to grind into a few cakes, then several. Given time, she would yandy the harvest of a broad plain.*
> Seven Sisters

Yank: Someone from the United States (see also *seppo*).

> *"She's a Yank," someone called, as if that would explain why a woman could possess such exceptional vehicular skills.*
> Woman Alone

Yankunytjatjara: (Aboriginal.) A language group in the central region of Australia.

> *A Yankunytjatjara boy crept over to help.*
> The Family Made of Dust

Yeah: Expression meant to prompt a response.

> *"Real criminal types, yeah?"*
> The Family Made of Dust

Yellow box: A type of eucalypt tree that is thought to be the best native tree for honey production.

> *When they had talked for a time, Gabe offered her a jar of yellow-box honey and set the message stick on the table.*
> The Family Made of Dust

For more information, see *Amazing Australia*.

For recipes, see *Fairy Bread and Bush Tucker*.

Yirrkala: An indigenous Arnhem Land community in the Northern Territory; also the people who live on that land.

> *"I know a woman from the Yirrkala, a tribe in Kakadu. She lives north of here now, out in the desert."*
> The Family Made of Dust

Yobbo: Uncouth person.

> *"Dad's not here heaps of the time, so my brother's supposed to take care of me," she said. "But he's always out runnin' with his yobbo friends."*
> The Family Made of Dust

Yulara: A small town in the Northern Territory.

> *Alcoholic beverages were allowed on Yulara only as a special concession for tourists.*
> Woman Alone

For more information, see *18,000 Miles*.

Z

Zack: Five cents.

Zebra crossing: Crosswalk.

Zebra finch: A tiny bird common in arid wooded areas that can survive harsh conditions.

> *As they worked, a flock of zebra finches twittered softly.*
> *The sound drifted down like manna.*
> The Family Made of Dust

For more information, see *Amazing Australia*.

Zed: The letter Z.

Ziff: A beard.

Zip your gob: (Imperative.) Shut your mouth; shut up (see *gob*).

Zonk: Idiot.

Zonked: Tired; drunk; overworked.

Free Sample from
Woman Alone
A Six-Month Journey Through the Australian Outback

Introduction

SOME YEARS AGO, I did something that most people, depending on their taste for risk, might consider daring, adventurous, or idiotic. I chucked everything to spend six months camping—alone, as a woman—in the Australian Outback.

Sounds bold, maybe, unless you know that the life I had constructed stick by stick and day by day was empty. The college degree that suited my goals as a novelist left me unsuited to a wide range of income-producing options, so I had landed in a corporate job I utterly despised.

My depression wasn't clinical—I functioned well enough and held down a job and ate regularly and exercised—but I was anything except happy. Every morning I dragged myself into an office building where my peers viciously tore down the overweight woman on our team, invented horribly clever and horribly misogynistic nicknames for our boss (most of my peers were women), and gossiped endlessly about who was sleeping with whom and what that might mean for the woman's career advancement (never the man's).

I lived in a basement apartment with so many health and safety violations that the police officer who arrived when my car was broken into offered to report my landlord. I declined because I would have been forced to find another place I could afford, a tall order in the Washington, DC metropolitan area.

I had tons of friends and went out nearly every weekend but the bar scene and the punk rock scene and the all-night party/hookup scene and the hanging out at movie night getting stoned scene had grown stale even before I'd received my degree. I had already dedicated myself to becoming a writer but was too mentally exhausted to get much writing done.

And that was the real problem. Because I wasn't pursuing my true place in the world, the life I was leading—corporatized, industrialized, and in which everything I had ever been taught to want had been falsely glamorized—was killing me.

Something had to be done. What, I wasn't exactly sure. For a year, I reached out to my company's London office. My father's family is at least half Scotts-Irish, so the transfer would have opened up explorations into that side of my heritage.

By the time the foreign office's director made it clear—through a blunt, face-to-face conversation that materialized only because we both happened to arrive at the deserted Virginia office at six in the morning—that an offer would never be extended, my backup plan had already been funded with a fat savings account.

The idea was to knock around in the UK until the money ran out. I hoped to be there for a year but the expenses made it much more likely I would only wander for six months. I would see the sights, visit the rolling countryside, and work on losing as much of my tan as any self-respecting UK citizen. Who knew what might arise during that time? Where might I land?

I applied for a sabbatical and started packing. Anything I wouldn't truly need when...if...I returned to the US was sold off or given away. The rest was stored in my parents' basement. Even the car I had so lovingly restored, and into which I had sunk a feverish amount of money, was put up for sale. The Triumph was too temperamental to sit unattended for six hours let alone six months, so selling it was the best option.

As the final sixty days ticked away, something bizarre and unsettling happened. Time and again, I was visited by vivid dreams of kangaroos and the red desert. Over the course of a few weeks, the images went from foggy to sharply intense.

These dream-visions never came when I was deeply asleep. Instead they appeared like beautiful hallucinations whenever I was drowsing. Their gravitational pull caught at my heart. As I rose up out of each one, its threads and its images clung to me for minutes and then hours.

Finally I surrendered. All right, already! I'll go to Australia!

I knew nothing about the country or what I might do there. But one thing was clear: this journey I had decided to take had always been about the Outback...even before I'd started dreaming.

That was perfectly fine with me. I'd considered hiking through America's largest national parks for a year but I really wanted to leave the country. Rather than walk the UK's cliffs and moors, perhaps I could camp in the desert.

No matter how I spent my time in Australia, though, something was waiting for me. Something had grown tired of waiting and was reaching out. I bought the ticket.

The frenzied preparations that went with switching destinations began. My division head had already said the company would not guarantee that my position would be open when I returned. In my mind, there was no guarantee that I would return to that company or even to the US.

With less than two weeks to go, I took a nap on the couch. As I drifted closer toward sleep, I fell into a vision of astonishing clarity. My spirit soared over red desert plains where a few stunted trees dotted the broad earth. I swooped down toward a lone tree with a twisted black trunk. Its thin canopy cast jagged shadows over a corpse.

My corpse. I floated inches above it, peering at the face to be certain that it was me and that I was dead. A film of dust coated eyes that stared blankly at the sky.

The shock jolted me awake. I sat for a long time thinking about how clear and detailed the vision had been. Was this a warning? I was twenty-seven years old. Any trip a woman undertakes alone involves risks, and wandering through undeveloped regions in a foreign country would entail dangers of which I was ignorant. This wasn't supposed to be a suicide mission. Should I cancel the trip?

In a way, though, I was already dead. Returning to the life I had been living was unthinkable. The depression that weighed me down, the sheer grind of sameness at my job, the poisonous gossip and the stretch of similar days would never end unless something was done...done by me, and done for me.

I decided to go. Even if I died in the outback, for a few short months—and really for the first time in my life—I would have lived fully.

I told no one about the vision. Too many opinions had already been proffered about my plans. My parents were of course worried but knew it was hopeless to try to dissuade me. My friends thought it was great while pointing out the homes, children, and responsibilities that prevented them from undertaking the same type of journey. My department head didn't think I'd last more than two months before begging for my job back. Who would I tell?

Halfway through the journey, I would find that lonely, twisted tree. The events that would take place there would threaten my life and be entirely out of my control...until, that is, I made a choice.

A choice made by me. A choice made for me.

That experience and my choice would change me forever. After finding that tree, the rest of my time in the Outback would be different. It would feel less compelling, as if marking that milepost had accomplished everything I'd come to achieve.

Eventually I realized that it had marked the turning point I'd hoped to find. My life before that tree had been so flawed that the escape hatch had been hidden. Still I'd known, or my heart had known, that a new road would lead to more than just surviving in a salaried position, more than just getting through every day by keeping my head down and my mouth shut.

Only a dramatic and dangerous event could reveal that road. Only facing death allowed me to choose life.

Before I headed into the Outback, the many people who had confessed that they wanted to do something similar also said that their kids, their spouse, their mortgage, their whatever were insurmountable obstacles that prevented them from undertaking their own journeys.

The truth is that they were also making a choice. They were bypassing one dream in order to pursue or maintain a different dream they valued more. Before my sabbatical, I purged nearly all my material possessions. That left the entire world open to possibility…even the possibility that my life would end.

Not everyone can or should take such drastic steps. But people who allow other considerations to overshadow their dreams should let go of the vision or idea or concept that actually isn't their dream. Stability, raising a family, and cultivating a life that's filled with comfort and joy are all dreams that can be fulfilled…if the dreamers are willing to make conscious and informed choices.

No matter what your dream looks like, my wish is that the book you're holding right now provides the hope and inspiration to launch you onto your own path. In these pages, you'll find the usual traveler's stories brightly painted with the ways other people live. You'll read some of my comments and hear the thoughts of others. Along the way, perhaps you'll find an undiscovered part of yourself. Perhaps you'll mark your own milestone.

Turn the page with every hope for the person you can become.

You've just finished reading a free sample from
Woman Alone
A Six-Month Journey Through the Australian Outback

Free Sample from
Seven Sisters
Spiritual Messages from Aboriginal Australia

Seven Sisters

EVERY ABORIGINAL GIRL looked forward to her initiation, the rites that would make her into a woman. Although the transition would be a happy time, the girls couldn't help but worry. They wondered if they would be able to learn all the songs and remember the lessons. Their bodies would know when the time had come and would make physical changes all by themselves. That knowledge gave the girls some comfort.

Boys underwent their own initiations, of course, frightening rites of blood and pain. Not every child succeeded the first time. When one boy failed the man-making ceremony, the shame was more than he could bear. To soothe his humiliation, he loudly claimed that girls were weak because their initiation wasn't nearly as difficult.

A young woman who had just completed her own rites grew angry at his words. Women's lives held dangers and pains no man could comprehend. Why, a mother had died in childbirth only the year before. Was she supposed to think less of the men because they would never face that danger? Ridiculous!

Still, the comments buzzed in her mind like a horde of bushflies. She wondered if other boys or even men thought the woman-making rite was less valuable. After fretting over this for days, she told her sisters something shocking. She was going to ask the elders to make her into a man.

The youngest sister, a reed-thin girl with hair like the floss of a kapok tree, began to cry. She thought the ceremony would actually change her sister's body into that of a man. Even after the others convinced her that wouldn't happen, she would not be silent.

The boys will say it's not fair to compare them to an adult, she said. *They must see that girls are also strong. I will go with you!*

For a long moment, no one spoke. Then it was agreed: If one went, they all went. What one suffered they would all suffer. The seven sisters had been that way ever since their mother had pushed them into the world like a living chain of years.

As they walked back to camp, they didn't say another word. Just by looking at the girls, everyone knew something serious was about to happen. Mothers put aside their grinding rocks and grandmothers scooped up the babies. Men stopped repairing their weapons, and even the boys abandoned their games to tag along. By the time the sisters stood before the elders, the entire camp had gathered.

The senior men and women knew the girls as wards to be cared for, as young minds that were curious yet lacking in experience. The oldest sister had already done much for her people so she was allowed to speak. When she did, the elders couldn't believe they had heard her correctly.

Test us with the man-making ceremony, the oldest sister said again. *Let us prove we are equal to men.*

For many hours the council discussed the request. Even as darkness grew, no one moved to light the fires or prepare food. Finally the senior woman nodded. Their request would be granted. As the oldest sister joined the ensuing celebration, she felt the eyes of the sky spirits on her. Her request was so unusual even they wanted to know if she would succeed. She could only hope that she would endure.

For the next few days, the girls' uncles disappeared for hours at a time. When they wandered back, they pretended not to have been gone while everyone else pretended not to have noticed their absence. One day the uncles left for only a short time. Then they leapt out of the bush shouting war cries.

The girls' mother and aunts grabbed the sisters in trembling arms. The men tugged and shoved intent on breaking the sisters free. It was time to change. Separating the children from everything they had ever known was the first step.

When the oldest sister's head was covered with a dingo pelt, she plunged into a darkness she'd never known existed. Each girl would face the ordeal alone. Hands guided them roughly into a fast run and the mourning cries of their aunts fell behind. For them, the girls were already dead.

By the time they reached the bora ground, the ceremonial site, their feet were bloody from thorns and stones. A man sang a song they had never heard before then told the girls to sing. They stammered as best they could through the chant. When the pelts were finally removed, the sisters saw seeds and stones arranged to form a symbol important to men.

The evening decayed into a dark night. The uncles left. For the first time, the girls weren't surrounded by aunties who could explain every sound and warriors who could defend against every enemy. If they lit a fire to drive away their fears, they would fail. If they fled the bora ground in terror, they would fail. If they attempted to return to camp, they would shame their family.

Strangeness haunted the dark hours. Terrible howls rose out of the bush and the sound of running feet mysteriously went nowhere. A sudden snap of branches startled the girls; a rhythmic clapping like boomerangs tapping together drove thorns into their temples. None of it made sense and all of it was terrifying.

When the sun finally rose, the uncles returned looking as rested as ever. The sisters were ragged and had bunched tightly together. The men lined them up and counted; seven remained. The girls had passed the first test. They had controlled their fear.

Training began in earnest. The men recited stories and songs that spoke of a man's life, his duties and his pride. The sisters stood motionless as their lips were cut over and over with a sharp stone. The sun wheeled through its burning cycle but they were given no food. Water was offered only at dusk, and then only what could be held in the palm of a man's hand.

After days of this, the uncles brought a feast. Bush tomatoes and bush potatoes and witchetty grubs had been roasted on hot coals. The loin of a kangaroo dripped with juice and the drumsticks of a bustard let off a smoky steam. Although their stomachs ached, the sisters took only enough to sustain their lives. In times of famine, their discipline would serve the entire clan. They had passed the final test.

The uncles used the sharp stones to scratch their own arms. They gathered up their blood and sprinkled it over the initiates as they sang the last song. The sisters had become men.

As they left the bora ground—this time without the cloak of youthful ignorance—everything looked different. They had a new path in the world and saw things from a different perspective. The oldest sister had felt much the same after her initiation into the world of women. Now she saw the world with the eyes of a man and a woman.

A corroboree, a celebration, was held in their honor. The oldest sister felt joy and pride. A part of her stayed detached, though, as if her soul moved in an entirely different realm. She yearned to transform again. Before that happened, she would be with her tribe for one more night...and then forever after.

Toward dawn, the corroboree was still going strong. The sun touched the horizon, yet the stars glowed like brilliant crystals. The sun climbed higher but the stars would not be quenched. Then the sky spirits swept the seven sisters into the heavens where they became a new constellation. To this day, the Pleiades remind us that men and women, although different, are equally strong.

The Message of Seven Sisters

WE OFTEN JOKE ABOUT DIFFERENCES between the genders to diffuse a very real tension. Men evolved to understand the world physically: to set aside emotions until they have the luxury of processing them, to spend long hours tracking in silence, to pursue and defend. Women evolved to understand the world intuitively: to communicate during group activities, to notice nonverbal signals from the youngest in their care, to select ripe berries based on years of ingrained experience. No wonder there's trouble!

In ancient times, the elder council eased the tension. Senior men discussed how events might affect the prosperity of the clan and other tribes. Senior women considered the emotional and psychological needs of individuals and the group. Every aspect of the community's physical and spiritual health was balanced against the others.

The seven sisters are extraordinary because they balanced different kinds of knowledge within themselves. They understood both masculine and feminine, physical and spiritual. When they added the pains of men to their pains as women, their wisdom surpassed that of the elders before their bodies had ripened enough to marry.

Taking on both male and female knowledge is dangerous. It requires one body and mind to bear the suffering of two genders. Yet sometimes that's exactly what women do…they carry their own burdens while shouldering those of a man. Single mothers protect and nurture their children while unmarried women build lives alone. Husbands grow ill or stumble so wives carry them for a month, a year, a lifetime. Widows become their own mates.

Today we are integrating the knowledge of the elder council, of both genders, into every level of society. Our schools and universities burst with female teachers and professors. Our businesses recognize the unique benefits of feminine leadership. Our highest courts understand that women from all backgrounds are wise, that their histories and experiences are critical to true justice.

Valuing women's perspectives has an additional benefit: it allows us to more fully value the contributions of men. In tribal structures, a man's reputation was based on what he did for the community. The best hunter and the highest earner provide no value if they hoard what they have hunted. Today, men who cannot achieve within a narrowly defined role are looked down on while "successful" men gobble up more than their share. Our modern society therefore does not truly honor a man's strengths and abilities.

When a man's identity is linked with iron chains to wealth or power, everyone suffers. Nations that focus only on tangible assets like economic stability and military strength lack the intangible assets of compassion and empathy. There is no use for grain stored in such vast quantities that it rots; there is no value to money horded in such quantities that it exists only as a numeric concept. A balanced society will distribute excess grain to those in need. A balanced person will utilize excess funds to bolster community projects.

The negative cycle of gender imbalanced is linked in other ways, too. When women's contributions are devalued, the man who performs the ultimate acts of strength—being a single father, carrying a wife through illness, allowing compassion to enhance his leadership—walks a gauntlet of social ridicule. He is "weak," "soft," "pussy-whipped," "gay." Gender-based terms make him womanly and therefore ineffectual. His strength is neutered by a brawny line between the sexes. *Approach that line,* men are told, *and become less than you were.*

The most important message from the Pleiades is that our natural state is one of mutual strength. The oldest sister did not want to physically become a man or to fulfill only a man's role. Nor did she seek to place women above men. Disenfranchising the men would have been as destructive as disenfranchising the women. Any society that values either gender more than the other is a society divided.

Back in the early days of the Dreamtime, the sisters were honored for their unique accomplishment. Despite having earned that respect, they had to be removed from the ancient world. Their dual perspective would have made their lives unbearable. Other women would not have been able to understand their knowledge of men; men would not have been able to relate to them as they did to other women. Their unique viewpoint would have caused the sisters an excessive amount of suffering.

Modern society has the opportunity to do what the sisters could not. During the last century, women and men have taken on each other's knowledge. Single parents, people who delay marriage or choose not to marry, widows and widowers have learned how to be protector and nurturer, provider and comforter. Now we can welcome people who hold this dual perspective. We can let their strength shine like stars burning among us.

This is the sacred message both genders have known since people first gathered into groups…that either gender can bear the burden for both. That the hearts of men and women are big enough and their arms are strong enough to carry a spouse, a family, a friend. This deeply spiritual love disappears only when we agree to hide it away. We are weak only when we choose to believe the modern myths that spring from issues of power and control, insecurity and instability.

These issues affect every nation in our modern world. In the U.S., much is made of the fact that religious restrictions in some countries bar women from receiving an education. Yet American fundamentalists from several popular religions bar women from becoming spiritual leaders or heads of household. Unwed mothers are maligned while absentee fathers, who conveniently bear no overt signs of their "sins," are spared any repercussions.

Our secular society is still influenced by these judgments. Education means little if it can never be used; employment is psychologically degrading when the wage gap between genders exceeds twenty percent; a woman making a bid for president is merely a footnote when few corporations have any female executives.

Yet the issue is not solely based in gender dynamics. Not when a college degree costs six figures, not when blue-collar workers are indentured by low wages and lower status. Domestic violence—against husbands and wives, children and elders—is driven in part by an economic model that pays too little for many people to support their families. The poorest among us are disenfranchised by a system that doesn't respect the contributions of every person.

Our societies have changed from tribes to nations, from neighborhoods to a global community. We are each responsible for improving our own society so it can improve the world. We are also responsible for sharing what we can with our far-flung neighbors. Our foreign sisters do not deserve fewer rights simply because they were born into systems mired in issues of power and control; our worldwide brothers also deserve to have their contributions fully valued.

In times of darkness, we need only look up to remember our power. The Pleiades, burning brightly for millennium, honor the sisterhood of mankind and the brotherhood of humanity. The way requires suffering, some of it harsh, and we will sometimes have to bear each others' burdens. Together we can celebrate equality and strength. Together we can lift free of our individual bodies. Together we can shine.

You've just finished reading a free sample from
Seven Sisters
Spiritual Messages from Aboriginal Australia.

Free Sample from
The Family Made of Dust
A Novel of Loss and Rebirth in the Australian Outback

1 The Precious Dead

WHEN A MAN DIES IN THE DESERT, he is completely alone. At thirty-nine, Ian McCabe knew this simple fact. He had spent most of his life working the demanding seasonal jobs that kept Australia's rural towns alive. He had seen a flat tire turn deadly, and knew that beauty and danger were the sisters who bore the land.

Ian was not a tall man but a shock of blond hair added inches to his height. Quick blue eyes and a steady aim were useful in his career as a kangaroo culler. Every night the slim .22 found its target between the shine of an animal's eyes. On cattle stations hundreds of kilometers wide, engine trouble and the bite of the brown snake posed constant threats.

Ian's white Land Rover was nearly twenty years old and it still ran like a lizard drinking—non-stop and practically unstoppable. In the rear a skillet, bedroll and a case of green beans were strapped onto narrow shelves. A bottle of port nestled in its own padded compartment, and a few golf clubs were tied to the wall. Sleep, slurp and sport, he called the collection, everything a man could want in one mobile space.

He eased the truck down the track. The spur was rough, really a strip of earth scraped clean of boulders, but it saved nearly half an hour. Besides, the less traveled a road was, the happier Ian felt. Cities, he knew, were for suckers. Why squeeze into a rabbit hutch when the outback was right next door?

This area, so close to the Davenport Ranges, was typical of the Northern Territory. Wide plains of twisted mulga trees reached southwest to Alice Springs. A network of creeks and rivers that ran only during the Wet sustained gum trees taller than most buildings. Cockatoos raised their young in the hollow trunks, and after a rain lorikeets gorged on the nectar in the blossoms.

Grass was sparse, edged out by the ubiquitous spinifex that cut flesh as cruelly as broken glass. Only the toughest creatures survived and half-feral Brahma cattle were the breed of choice. To a rancher beleaguered by drought and debt, every blade eaten by native animals robbed them of beef. Roo shooters were always welcome. And judging by the sun, Ian would arrive at the station house in time for dinner.

A flash of metal caught his eye. Through binoculars, he watched a red SUV beetle across the property. The truck stayed behind the ridges and moved slowly enough to keep its dust cloud low. The same stealth kept Ian from sight as he followed.

Eventually the trespassers parked beside a hill topped by a stone pinnacle. Ian stuffed the Land Rover under a mulga tree and watched as a pair of men hiked up the slope. The first, a sturdy white fellow about thirty years old, clutched a rifle. His legs were bowed so severely he rocked as he mounted the boulders.

The other man, an Aborigine who might have been in his sixties, moved steadily upward. He was wiry yet had the grace of a predator. The outback was filled with men like them, drifters who found the bush far removed from the law.

At the top, the elder found a cleft in the rock. From this cache he retrieved a board nearly as long as his arm. Ian had seen dancers perform with similar objects and knew they were supposed to be magical. The cubby surrendered perhaps a dozen other artifacts. All would fetch a small fortune on the black market.

While the older man worked steadily, the bowlegged bloke couldn't keep a proper watch. First he rubbed his nose with the back of his arm. Then he adjusted his shorts. He scanned the landscape, rifle at ready. Then he swatted a fly. Rubbed sweat through his hair. Tugged at his crotch. Abruptly he was alert again, scowling while the gun grew hot in the sun.

As they retreated, the Aborigine erased his footprints with a leafy branch. Ian let the SUV jangle out of sight before picking up the trail. They traveled faster now and corkscrewed across their original path. Where the spur intersected a paved road dusty tread marks headed toward the Stuart Highway, the only paved north-south road through the Territory. The pair could pick from dozens of unmarked byways. The artifacts would disappear.

Ian pushed the Land Rover to its limit. Although the old truck handled beautifully in the bush, it was as sluggish as a fly in winter. The needle was still climbing when Ian saw the red SUV parked beside the highway. If he pulled over, the men would surely notice when he followed them later.

The Toyota, a new model free of dents or scrapes, faced the road. The younger man smirked and the lines around his mouth twisted. Again Ian was struck by the elder's expression. White pipe clay severed his forehead and chin, and his face was a jigsaw of violence.

"So you've seen me," Ian murmured, "and I've seen you." He adjusted the rearview mirror but couldn't make out the tag number.

A roadhouse a quarter-hour away was a convenient place to watch for the men but they never appeared. It was possible they had turned east toward the coast. More likely they had dodged off into the bush. As night covered the sky, Ian had plenty of time to consider his next action.

He didn't need a fraction of it. The kangaroos could wait.

***

THOUSANDS OF KILOMETERS TO THE EAST, Gabriel Branch loaded the last of his bags into the hatchback. At six feet tall, Gabe barely fit behind the wheel even with the seat pushed all the way back. But the rear compartment was roomy enough to hold all his diving gear, and the hatch was easier to use than a station wagon. He squeezed in and steered for the coastal highway out of Townsville.

The next few days would be spent an hour or so south on the Whitsunday Islands. In the forty-five years Gabe had lived in Queensland, he rarely traveled more than a hundred kilometers inland. The neighbors never quite understood why his vacations didn't take advantage of the expansive desert at their back doors.

They didn't understand the...complications of Gabe's life. Oh, they knew about the Aboriginal land rights issues that had consumed the media for decades, and had heard about the children adopted by white families in a long-defunct effort to assimilate the race. But they didn't know what it was like to be caught by those issues against their will. Only a biracial Aborigine who had been assimilated at the age of three could tell them that. And Gabe wasn't talking.

Nor was he interested in drawing attention. Black faces were scarce in Australia, so he stuck close to the coastal cities that hosted international travelers in all their rainbow colors. He blended in better there and no one asked many questions about his background. Even when they did, they were met with silence.

Silence had kept his life on the smooth, orderly track he worked so hard to create. Last week he had hit a bump—a big bump—in his relationship with a Jamaican woman. Chance hadn't been in the country more than a few years. But she had some definite ideas about how much Gabe should say about his experiences and how loudly his voice should sound.

They had fought about it more of late. He supposed it was the same with all couples, as if money or household chores or work schedules were the cause of their problems instead of a symptom. Whatever the real reason, Gabe and Chance had split up last week. The separation was supposedly temporary, just a little breathing and thinking room, but Gabe knew where that would lead.

If Ian had been available, Gabe would have talked things over with him. In fifteen years of friendship, the men had seen each other through a number of breakups. None had been as serious as this one, though, and Gabe wished Ian would call. He already missed Chance's rapid-fire commentary and her odd machinegun laugh. Before the split, Gabe had been thinking of proposing. But courage in one person required courage in the other. And that, he knew, was the real reason their separation would be permanent.

When Ian did call, Gabe was already out of range. He heard only the clack of sugar cane as he sped past the coastal farms.

***

IAN TRACKED THE MEN FOR DAYS without coming within twenty kilometers of the truck. The outback was so big and its population so small, a little luck and a few calls let him keep tabs on the thieves as they passed through different roadhouses. At a tourist site called Devil's Marbles, a vendor remembered the odd pair and pointed to a faint track heading west.

When he located the Toyota, he parked some distance away and hiked in for a better look. Perhaps a dozen coffins had been removed from crevices in a wadi. The thieves were stealing bodies. Ian trotted back to the Land Rover and gunned the engine, all but honking to make sure they heard as he rattled toward the ridge.

The thieves took the hint. After the Toyota disappeared, Ian walked into the gully to inspect the damage. The coffins, each a cradle for the precious dead, were lined up in the center. Tarps and coils of rope had been left behind, along with cigarette butts and candy wrappers. The urine drying on the cliff face still smelled sharp.

Then Ian spotted the truck tucked under a ledge. It was the same one he had seen leave, he was sure of it. The guano he had noticed days earlier was still smeared on the side window. Yet the culvert had no other entrance except the one he had just walked through.

A bullet spun him off his feet. He heard nothing, not even the echo of the shot, as his shirt soaked in a red tide. The blood was brilliant at first, like the eyes of the metallic starlings that congregated around his boyhood home. He saw the Aborigine kneel beside him as his breath fled past his tongue.

The man was older than he had thought, much older, and carried with him the aura of ancient things. He wore only a string belt, a pair of shorts, and bands on his arms and legs. Tufts of cockatoo feathers framed a radiant face. On his chest a swirl of dots and circles, made hypnotic by his breath, pulled Ian into a galaxy of red.

He was terribly confused. He tried to separate the ringing in his head from his memories. They ran away, he thought. He had seen them drive across the plateau that drained west of the escarpment, had watched them until they were out of sight. The tire tracks he had crossed floated in his mind. Only one set of tracks, he realized. The truck had never left. How could he have been so wrong?

As if to offer comfort, the elder caressed Ian's forehead. The man's hair, shot with gray, looked nutmeg. It was as if his great age had worn the shine off the strands and leached away the pigment. His eyes were luminous, though, beyond the touch of time. Ian thought of the dingoes that gazed into his spotlight. The dogs always waited, knowing he would leave the kangaroo's heart and liver and kidneys for their feast.

Suddenly he understood. This man was a shaman. Ian had been lured into the culvert just as he had been tricked into speeding down the highway. He smiled and reached up.

"There, now," the man soothed, and flicked his blade across Ian's throat.

You've just finished reading a free sample from
The Family Made of Dust
A Novel of Loss and Rebirth in the Australian Outback.

About the Author

Laine Cunningham is an award-winning author, ghostwriter and publishing consultant who has been quoted on CNN, MSNBC.com, and FoxNews.com.

Her novels interweave social, cultural, historical, political and spiritual movements that have occurred within different groups and at different time periods. These elements are intended to engage readers in discussions of how similar forces have changed or are changing the contemporary world...and what might lie in our future.

Her nonfiction books range from memoirs to self-help and business humor. A series of writing and publishing books have been produced under Writer's Resource, the writing and publishing consultancy she has owned and operated for twenty years.

Also by Laine Cunningham

Nonfiction

Seven Sisters
Spiritual Messages from Aboriginal Australia
For readers of *The Secret*, *A Course in Miracles*, and Paul Coelho's works. *Seven Sisters* harnesses Dreamtime energy to help modern people address their challenges. In this collection of essays, readers discover that love and friendship, parenting, life and the afterlife can be addressed with the unchanging wisdom of the human heart.
"Intoxicating ... enlightening ... mesmerizing and meaningful."
– Hall of Fame Top Reviewer

Woman Alone
A Six-Month Journey Through the Australian Outback
For fans of Cheryl Strayed's *Wild* and
Elizabeth Gilbert's *Eat, Pray, Love*.
Laine Cunningham seemed to have it all, yet every morning she dragged herself through a falsely glamorized life. Guided only by a map pulled from an old copy of *National Geographic*, she camped in the Australian Outback for six months...and she did it alone.
Told with wry humor and sparked with suspense and warmth, *Woman Alone* conveys a desperate search that became a journey of comedy and compassion in a landscape that brought her peace.

Writing While Female or Black or Gay
Diverse Voices in Publishing
A provocative and polarizing—yet often deadly funny—look behind the scenes of the publishing industry. The empowerment of Tina Fey's *Bossy Pants*, the warmth of Amy Poehler's *Yes Please*, the sensibilities of Wanda Sykes, and the strength of Mindy Kaling's *Is Everyone Hanging Out Without Me?* come together in a narrative that mirrors the polemic language of Caitlin Moran's *How to Be a Woman*.
"Truthful and caustic and sensible." Vine Voice Top Reviewer

18,000 Miles
An Australia Travel Guide Companion to Woman Alone
For readers who want to delve deeper into the 18,000-mile journey Laine relays in *Woman Alone,* this travel companion tells all. Where to sleep, which sites to visit, and how to access services are laid out in this informative work that tracks all the destinations from her six-month solo Outback journey.

Amazing Australia
A Traveler's Guide to Common Plants and Animals
Take a trip through the wild strangeness that earned Australia the nickname Oz. Information on common and unique animals and plants, including feral flora and fauna, covers everything you need to know to enjoy a trip to Australia.

Fairy Bread and Bush Tucker
Surviving a Gastronomical Adventure in Australia (With Recipes)
Every country claims its own cuisine, some of which can seem bizarre or downright disgusting. Learn about the best and worst foods in Australia, and how to cook exact or similar dishes even when ingredients can't be found outside of the country.

Fiction

The Family Made of Dust
A Novel of Loss and Rebirth in the Australian Outback
When Gabriel Branch searches the outback for his best friend, he crosses paths with a tribal shaman who forces him to face the Aboriginal heritage he lost as a child. Fans of Sara Gruen's *Like Water for Elephants* and Sue Monk Kidd's *The Secret Life of Bees* will welcome this gripping, poignant debut novel ranked alongside Pulitzer greats William Styron and Horton Foote.
Winner of two national awards.
One of the best novels in ten years of running this contest.
– Hackney Literary Awards Committee

Beloved
A Noir Thriller
The dark Swedish noir of Erik Axl Sund's *The Crow Girl* shadows America's Allegheny Mountains in this atmospheric page-turner. A blistering police procedural and the FBI profiler hunt for two serial killers interweave in a complex novel compared to Steig Larsson's *The Girl with the Dragon Tattoo*. Recipient of three national honors.

Reparation
A Novel of Love, Devotion and Danger
A short vacation turns into a sinister game to save a sister from a peyote cult in this compulsive and compelling story about a Native American man. A profoundly moving story about the abiding love between siblings and the strength of romantic love, *Reparation* is both a gripping page-turner and an emotionally charged journey through the brittle first tendrils of love into the power—and destructive capabilities—of love in its many forms. Shortlisted for three national awards.

www.ingramcontent.com/pod-product-compliance
Lightning Source LLC
Chambersburg PA
CBHW070625300426
44113CB00010B/1666